Capacity Planning
with SAP®

Uwe Göhring

Thank you for purchasing this book from Espresso Tutorials!

Like a cup of espresso coffee, Espresso Tutorials SAP books are concise and effective. We know that your time is valuable and we deliver information in a succinct and straightforward manner. It only takes our readers a short amount of time to consume SAP concepts. Our books are well recognized in the industry for leveraging tutorial-style instruction and videos to show you step by step how to successfully work with SAP.

Check out our YouTube channel to watch our videos at
https://www.youtube.com/user/EspressoTutorials.

If you are interested in SAP Finance and Controlling, join us at
http://www.fico-forum.com/forum2/
to get your SAP questions answered and contribute to discussions.

Related titles from Espresso Tutorials:

- ▶ Claudia Jost: First Steps in the SAP® Purchasing Processes (MM)
  http://5016.espresso-tutorials.com
- ▶ Björn Weber: First Steps in the SAP® Production Processes (PP)
  http://5027.espresso-tutorials.com
- ▶ Stephen Birchall: Invoice Verification for SAP®
  http://5073.espresso-tutorials.com
- ▶ Kevin Riddell, Rajen Iyver: Practical Guide to SAP® GTS, Part 1: SPL Screening and Compliance Management
  http://5100.espresso-tutorials.com
- ▶ Avijt Dutta & Shreekant Shiralkar: Demand Planning with SAP® APO—Concepts and Design
  http://5105.espresso-tutorials.com
- ▶ Avijt Dutta & Shreekant Shiralkar: Demand Planning with SAP® APO—Execution
  http://5106.espresso-tutorials.com
- ▶ Tobias Götz, Anette Götz: Practical Guide to SAP® Transportation Management (2nd edition)
  http://5082.espresso-tutorials.com
- ▶ Matthew Johnson: SAP® Material Master—A Practical Guide
  http://5028.espresso-tutorials.com

Uwe Göhring
Capacity Planning with SAP®

ISBN:	978-1-5464-8971-9
Editor:	Karen Schoch
Cover Design:	Philip Esch
Cover Photo:	istockphoto.com # 185010218 © rrocio
Interior Design:	Johann-Christian Hanke

All rights reserved.

1st Edition 2017, Gleichen

© 2017 by Espresso Tutorials GmbH

URL: *www.espresso-tutorials.com*

Feedback
We greatly appreciate any kind of feedback you have concerning this book. Please mail us at *info@espresso-tutorials.com*.

Table of Contents

Introduction

Managing a company's resources is one of the biggest contributors to its success or failure, if not done well. And by managing, I mean the process of planning, allocating, sequencing, leveling and scheduling these resources so that they provide us with the best possible utilization or 'bang for our buck'. Resources, in this context, include machines, laborers, entire production lines, tools, storage facilities, processing tanks and much more.

Planning of these resources is often neglected, considered pointless or deemed unnecessary. In many companies, product inventories and expected sales figures are projected with great care, but ensuring the appropriate level of resource availability is more of an afterthought. The 'fire-fighting' approach seems to be the strategy of choice (even though it's hardly a strategy) and managers simply accept that in order to run a production floor, you must deal with an exorbitant amount of exceptions.

I disagree. Resources can and must be planned for. In other areas, it is done very well. If there is enough pressure to avoid failure and the accountability is clear, a plan is executed that ensures the least amount of deviation. Take the airline industry, for example. Imagine you have just boarded a flight and sat down in an aisle seat. The captain and co-pilot are talking with the board engineer and the crew in the middle aisle about the weight and balance of the airplane. The discussion might go something like this:

Flight attendant: "Today we have 80 passengers, which fills the plane to 65%."

Pilot: "How's the weight distributed?"

Flight attendant: "Most of them are seated at the front of the cabin."

Engineer: "If the weight isn't distributed evenly, we might crash into the forest at the end of the runway because we can't take off... and if we take off, we might experience really disruptive flight behavior by the airplane."

Co-Pilot: "Yeah, I had that on a flight into Fort Lauderdale last year and we had to rig the airplane nose up for the entire flight, which burned so much fuel we almost ran out."

Pilot: "That's not good... so let's see how we can distribute the passengers a bit... how about the luggage below?"

Flight attendant: "That's done, but I don't know where they put it."

Pilot: "Hey guys, that's really scary but we have to get these passengers to their destination, otherwise we'll get a bad track record for poor on-time delivery. Let's just go and hope for the best."

I don't think you would want to overhear a conversation like that. And don't worry, this kind of talk never happens on an airplane (I hope) because flight crews are obligated to plan ahead, anticipate what could happen and put policies in place for eventualities. But why do we only do that when lives are on the line? Can't we take financial and competitive situations seriously enough to warrant good planning?

I dare you to take a long, hard look at your planning system and compare it to that of the situation described above. There is no excuse for not reserving capacity, balancing the production line, evenly spreading out the work (whether it comes in exactly like you anticipated or not), putting buffers in place (inventory, capacity and time) by which you quote delivery times, and working with a set of policies that enable you to operate at the edge of your possible performance boundaries—no matter which situation plays out later.

Be prepared, it pays off regardless of whether lives are saved or 'only' your customer service is improved.

Whether you plan well or you are looking to improve your capacity management, the aim of this book is to illuminate an otherwise largely neglected and rarely used function in SAP. In my experience, during the implementation of SAP software, capacity management is almost always put on the 'back burner' and is rarely picked up on after the go-live chaos recedes.

I hope the following provides you with some inspiration to improve resource planning with SAP. I am convinced that it's well worth the effort.

Uwe Goehring, New York, NY, January 24, 2017

We have added a few icons to highlight important information. These include:

Tips

 Tips highlight information that provides more details about the subject being described and/or additional background information.

Attention

 Attention notices highlight information that you should be aware of when you go through the examples in this book on your own.

Finally, a note concerning the copyright: all screenshots printed in this book are the copyright of SAP SE. All rights are reserved by SAP SE. Copyright pertains to all SAP images in this publication. For the sake of simplicity, we do not mention this specifically underneath every screenshot.

1 Capacity Management in SAP ERP

What is the essence of capacity planning? What improvements and results does it produce and what opportunities arise from it? In this chapter, you will gain an understanding of the functionality around capacity planning, sequencing, leveling and scheduling. I will explain the various options you have in terms of leveling your resources from a business point of view. I will explore the history and evolution of material requirements planning (MRP) to MRPII and advanced planning systems (APS), and what role capacity planning plays in the attempt to build a better supply program. I'll wrap up by taking a look at the areas where capacity planning is used within the context of SAP.

Capacity management is the process organizations use to ensure resources meet current and future business requirements to manufacture a product or provide a service. A resource, in this context, may be human, a machine that provides hours of operative time, an oven that offers cubic meters of space to cook, or a continuous assembly line that runs at various production rates to make a product at a speed that conforms to a predefined 'takt' time.

Takt

'Takt' is the German word for speed, beat or timing. So, takt time is 'beat time', 'rate time' or 'heart beat'. Lean production uses takt time as the rate that a completed product needs to be finished in order to meet customer demand.

Capacity management is the art of planning, sequencing, leveling, and scheduling jobs that are required to most effectively meet demand. Capacity management not only happens at the supply gate (more about gates later), but may also be used to roughly check a demand plan for available resources in long-term planning for simulations, and for planned orders in MRP. Capacity management—if applied properly—can vastly improve the supply plan.

1.1   Using science in operations and capacity management

SAP software is typically implemented using blueprints, templates and guidelines which have little to do with methods and theories employed in the science of operations planning. Many people still think that there is no such thing as a science for operations or capacity planning. However, extensive literature on the subject delivers proof that methods and theories have been around for a long time. Maybe the problem is that a scientific framework of operational science does not fit in with the buzzwords abounding in recent years in the disciplines of supply chain management.

Works such as Eliyahu Goldratt's 'The Goal' and his associated Theory of Constraints, Wallace and Hopp's book 'Factory Physics' and John Sterman's excellent elaboration on the subject of 'Thinking in Systems' are considered old ideas in supply chain terms. However, people still read them and discuss the subject matter, but the resulting principles, laws and corollaries are rarely applied to the way we use SAP as a tool to manage, plan and execute our operations.

What is alarming, however, is the fact that for almost everything, from engineering to product development, we apply science to achieve predictable and desired results. Take for example prototyping and designing of new automobiles. Clearly, an automotive company does some market research before they build a new car, and they derive requirements from that research. It could happen that customers look for bigger cars with, say, 1000 kilograms of mass. Potential buyers may also want a car that can accelerate at 2.7 meters per second squared (0 to 60 in 10 seconds). But to keep the cost low and the car at an affordable sales price, the engine in the new automobile can produce no more than 200 newtons of force (see Figure 1.1).

Naturally, you would use Newton's second law of motion to figure out if it's possible to make a car which meets these requirements. Newton's law states: 'The vector sum of the external forces F on an object is equal to the mass m of that object multiplied by the acceleration vector a of the object: $F = ma$'.

12

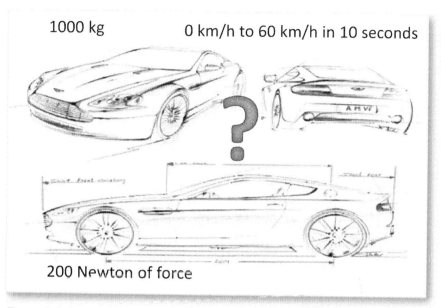

Figure 1.1: Requirements for the design of a new automobile

Applying this formula, we can immediately see that the requirements are impossible to fulfill because a mass of 1000 kilograms requires far more force than 200 newtons to accelerate the car from zero to a speed of 60 kilometers per hour in 10 seconds, as can be seen in Figure 1.2.

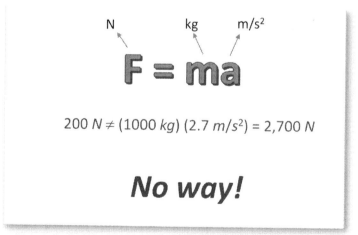

Figure 1.2: Newton's second law of motion applied

On the other hand, when it comes to management and planning of operations and our resources, we traditionally base decisions on experience and intuition and not on science. Good intuition can be an extremely efficient guide to making good decisions, and is primarily developed out of a solid scientific reference framework. Experience must also be of the right kind. What good is experience gained from many years of making bad decisions?

Let's now look at how people usually design the way in which their factories and operations are run. For example, if a plant requires an output of 3000 manufactured units per day, with a lead time of not greater than 10 days and with a service level (percent of jobs that finish on time) of at least 90%, how do we know if this can be achieved? A good manager with lots of experience can probably tell you. However, the actual problem lies in the fact that if it turns out that these requirements can't be met, there may be no one who knows how to actually fulfill the demand. Things get more complicated when demand and supply variability enter the mix. People then look at high inventory values and frequent stockouts and everybody scrambles around to find ways to fix the situation.

If you know that variability is best reduced with the optimal combination of the three buffers which develop when variability is present (time, inventory, capacity), and you understand the dynamics that Little's Law (work in process = throughput x cycle time) describes, you can clarify the problem and take action to resolve it.

To illustrate this situation, let's have a look at 'flow benchmarking'—a scientific framework developed by the people at Factory Physics. In flow benchmarking, you plot the components of Little's Law in order to benchmark a product line's performance (the same can be done for a plant or an entire supply chain). Figure 1.3 shows an example of flow benchmarking (the example omits cycle time).

The solid, red line (rising steeply then flattening out) represents the greatest possible output with the given capacity the line can operate with. It therefore assumes the line runs at full capacity utilization without any variability degrading performance. However, without a minimum work in process (WIP) level within the system, the line cannot produce the full throughput. This is identified by the rising solid, red line before it flattens out and reaches its maximum at the minimum WIP level. However, throughput cannot then increase any further, no matter how much more WIP, or inventory, you put into the system.

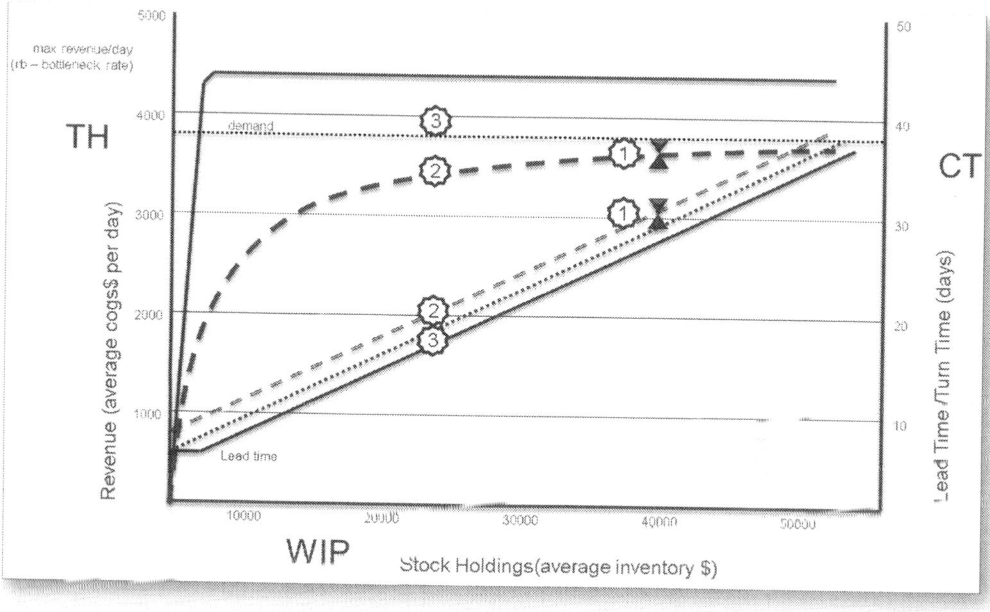

Figure 1.3: Flow benchmarking with Little's Law

The black, dashed line represents a sub-optimal state and assumes that significant variability exists. This line clearly shows that the full capacity utilization can only be achieved when the WIP (inventory) level is increased dramatically. You can now determine where you stand in this diagram by putting a plot point at the intersection of your own throughput and how much WIP you count in your system. Should you find yourself somewhere between the dashed and solid line, you're in the 'lean zone' and as long as you meet demand, all is well. However, if your plot point is found towards the right and below the dashed line, some optimization efforts would be of value to your company.

Flow benchmarking also helps you to define your improvement activities because if you find yourself at plot point (1), as seen in Figure 1.3, simply reducing inventory moves you straight down to the left on the dashed line and can drastically reduce your throughput. That is an unfavorable result for your career. A better way would be to reduce inventory towards plot point (2) and simultaneously design some buffering strategies to

15

reduce variability and use better scheduling methods which would move your performance straight up to plot point (3). This means that you increase throughput with less WIP *and* cover the existing demand.

Using this scientific framework, you can make far better decisions than with experience and intuition alone. Some of these decisions are made at the time of SAP software implementation, others are made later during the use of it. Furthermore, if you take a close look at how most SAP implementations are conducted, you may recognize that the nature of the implementation does not have very much to do with any scientific theory or sound idea on how to gain sustainability and efficiency. You might argue that SAP works with a certain modus operandi. Is this really true? Isn't SAP the tool which provides options that can be customized to our specific process, rather than being the 'way' we have to conduct our business? Doesn't SAP software provide a very large toolbox of options from which we can pick one to fit our operations? Who says you must use discrete production orders for your manufacturing operations? What is the logic behind using the same component availability checking rules across the board? Why do people say that the only way in SAP to achieve pull is by way of eKanban?

There are decisions made during the implementation that are based on rumors, hearsay, guesswork and loose assumptions but certainly not on knowledge or a scientific basis which could lead us to better setups and subsequently better results. Take, for example, the process of planning for finished goods sold through a product catalog. Almost all SAP customers I have seen would set up the product with standard strategy group 40 and then the sales representative would input sales orders using transaction VA01. In it, the availability check sometimes produces a delivery proposal and if it does, the representative doesn't always fully understand the implications for the production line when confirming or fixing the date. Should they fix the date? Should the quantity and proposed delivery date be confirmed to the customer? What happens in the planning department? How is the forecast consumed (if it even is consumed)? Can we learn from the fact that we couldn't deliver on time? (what was the forecast accuracy?) Where is the source of the problem causing us not to deliver and how can we improve for next time?

Answering these questions requires a reference framework with performance boundaries and a toolbox full of functionality so you can react flexibly to efficiency-degrading variability and ever-changing market conditions. To develop the framework, we can use science and to fill the toolbox with functions, we have to understand what functions the standard SAP system provides and how these functions work—way above and beyond what can be covered and dealt with during an implementation.

1.2 Dealing with conflicting goals

Have you ever wondered why your continuous improvement program feels like you are going around circles? This might be because you have to deal with conflicting goals. You can only increase profitability if a clear direction and strategy is identified and put into action. This direction requires an understanding of what happens when a company is made up of different interest groups who try to achieve potentially differing goals.

On one hand, costs need to be reduced and on the other, we need to increase revenue, profits or sales. To reduce costs, companies usually strive to reduce working capital (work in process, stocks, resources etc.) and save on the cost of procurement or production. They optimize their planning processes so that they can be executed more efficiently. In order to achieve the expected result, you require low inventories in raw, semi-finished and finished goods, high utilization of resources and less variability in demand and supply.

The other side of the coin is the desired increase in sales, which can be achieved with fast responses to customers' wishes, on-time delivery, very high quality with less waste and scrap, and the offer of a wide variety of options and customized features in the finished product. Logically, this requires ample supply of all variants of the finished good and ample capacity on the production lines so rush orders can be attended to quickly, and results in a lot of variability (see Figure 1.4).

Due to these conflicting goals, companies often become bipolar in their efforts for continuous improvement. Should we reduce inventory or increase availability? Cut down on our offering of product options, or offer more? Fully load our production lines, or run them at a fraction of their capacity?

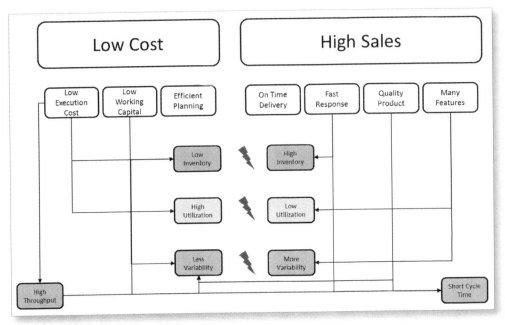

Figure 1.4: Conflicting goals

The key is to find the perfect balance. Practical science such as 'Factory Physics' (based on the book by Mark Spearman and Wallace Hopp) provides a great framework to find that balance. In Factory Physics, tools such as the flow optimizer or efficiency curve, in conjunction with the application of Little's Law, the VUT equation (which relates the Inventory, Capacity and Time buffers) and the determination of the Variance in Lead Time Demand help greatly to optimize capacity, WIP, inventory and cash flow and to determine the policies that support the strategy your company is aiming for.

It is these policies that we need to define for the SAP supply chain. With policy, we can execute a given supply chain strategy. It represents the planner's toolset to react to changing situations and to counter variability. The more standard policies you put in your toolbox, the more flexibly, agilely and efficiently you will operate and reach your goals.

It is far outside the scope of this book to describe the details on how to use Factory Physics to derive effective policies, but we strongly suggest doing more research on the subject and finding a way to develop a reference framework for yourself and your company.

1.3   What is capacity management?

Capacity management is the process of making an operations plan feasible for execution in terms of its required and available resources. Resources, in this case, include machines, work stations, humans, raw materials and purchased parts, and any tools and operating forms, jigs or riggings that may be needed to start and finish the production process.

Capacity is typically measured in available and required 'time' (hours, minutes or days). Essentially, capacity planning compares required time with available time and, as a result, provides you with utilization—a rate expressed as a percentage. A utilization of more than 100% is impossible to execute, even though many planners work this way. In fact, when utilization approaches 100%, execution becomes progressively more difficult when variability is present.

Capacity needs to be managed in the planning cycle. Not performing capacity checks, not re-scheduling or not making adjustments, results in a number of sub-optimal situations. Namely, raw materials' requirements dates are off, production orders get stuck on the line, work in process increases without bounds and you end up with exception messages galore. Sometimes the act of dealing with capacity is called *scheduling*. No matter what you call it, it is part of the planning cycle which includes the following activities: entering demand (planned or actual), planning the supply which ought to cover the demand, scheduling or capacity management, executing the orders, and finally, either holding the finished product in stock for sales or delivering the product directly to the customer. The planning cycle is depicted in Figure 1.5.

As we are focusing on capacity management, we can further detail the act of scheduling, as shown in Figure 1.6 In SAP terms, the planning part of the cycle is represented by the MRP Run (in the short term). It generates a supply plan (planned orders) using policy (master data settings) to cover demand (planned or actual), with absolutely *no* consideration of available (or not available) capacity. It is the responsibility of the scheduler or capacity planner to take capacity into consideration.

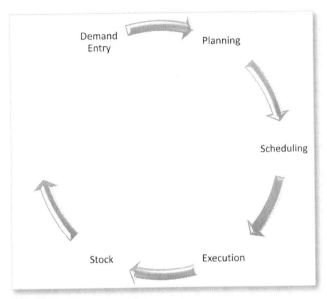

Figure 1.5: Planning cycle

Furthermore, that person is tasked with scheduling a pool of orders within a certain time frame. To do so, the orders first have to be put into a sequence according to some sort of criteria (maybe heijunka or setup optimization) and then leveled on the work centers or production line as available hours permit.

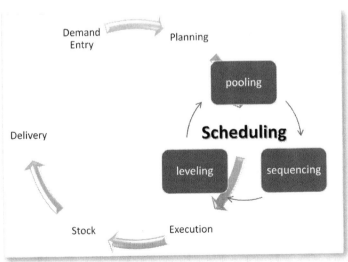

Figure 1.6: Scheduling in the planning cycle

You can think of this process as water running down from a holding pool and being channeled to various streams using a specific flow rate. Figure 1.7 illustrates this idea and if you look closely, you can see a mixed model line producing different colored liquids.

Figure 1.7: Scheduling water running down a waterfall

The importance of performing capacity management, scheduling orders and checking resources before the production lines are filled with orders cannot be stressed enough. Failing to do so results in an incomplete planning and execution process and does not produce the desired and expected results. Figure 1.8 gives some examples of the impact production scheduling (or the lack thereof) can have on the overall supply chain.

Low service levels due to orders piling up while they wait for room on the line, high work in process levels due to a lack of flow, long lead times to the customer and permanent stockouts are the norm in a system without proper capacity management.

Figure 1.8: The impact of production scheduling on the supply chain

Conversely, there are many factors from the other functions in the supply chain which require information from production scheduling. Sales or distribution want to know what they can promise to the customer, the materials planner needs to define economic lot sizes and other components of the replenishment policy, and management always wants to know about important production key performance indicators (KPIs).

As shown in Figure 1.9, a multitude of factors make it transparent and clear that without proper scheduling and capacity management, no company can survive in today's marketplace. And yet capacity management in SAP remains a mystery for many. It may be because during implementation, capacity management is considered an afterthought and is promised to be dealt with sometime later down the road.

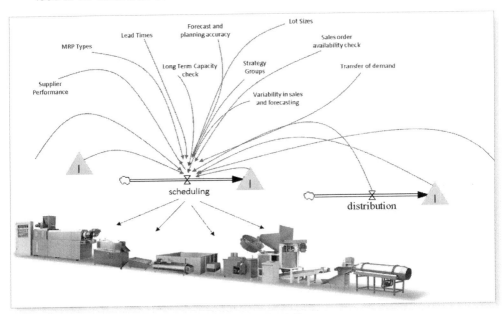

Figure 1.9: Factors influencing production scheduling

1.3.1 Capacity management phases

Capacity management is a term used to describe a sequenced system of repeatable tasks. Each and every one of these tasks serves to balance resource availability with the capacity load it has to cope with. In order to do so, capacity management can be broken down into the following phases:

- ▶ Planning
- ▶ Sequencing
- ▶ Leveling
- ▶ Scheduling
- ▶ Evaluation

When managing capacity, the sequence of the phases has to be adhered to, as do the individual tasks within the phases. First, you must plan the amount of capacity that is needed to execute the plan. Once available resources are set up and planned for, the resource load from orders has to be dealt with. Sequencing constitutes the first phase of load management and with it, orders within a specified time horizon are sorted according to a predefined sorting strategy. After the orders are put into a sequenced order, they are then dispatched in that sequence within the available capacity profile of the bottleneck work center or production line. We call this part *leveling,* because the capacity load is evened out within the time horizon in question. Once the orders are evenly distributed, a system (or person) can now schedule the order's basic dates. This is often done with backward scheduling, where an order's start date is determined by subtracting the order's lead time from the end date. Finally, some monitoring or evaluation activities take place in order to deal with exceptional situations and variability in the system.

Figure 1.10 shows the phases of capacity management.

After the operations plan is activated, the required capacity offering is planned for. It requires careful master data management. In SAP, there is the material master, the work center, the routing and various profiles which carry data for capacity management. The routing essentially includes data to calculate capacity requirements, whereas the work center is the place to identify capacity availability. To plan capacity, these two elements are crucial for decision making. Accurate and current data enable the development of policies and tactics.

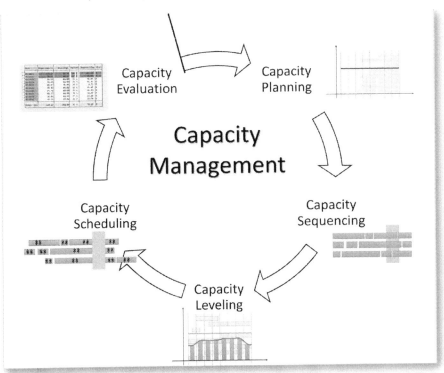

Figure 1.10: Phases of managing capacity

For sequencing, there are many options pre-configured in SAP. You can sort according to setup optimization, FIFO (first-in, first-out) or heijunka and there are many more that can be customized. For any given period, a sequence record is saved, which is used in the next step for the distribution within available capacity. Leveling uses the order's load and the work center's availability to figure out at what specific point in time the order will be placed.

Formulas stored in the work center record and strategies configured in customization then drive the scheduling of the orders in the plan, which concludes the cycle of capacity management, and the finite schedule can then be released to the production lines (after a collective component availability check). In the following section, I'll describe in more detail the individual phases of capacity management.

Capacity planning

Capacity planning in SAP is the act of providing enough resource availability to enable a given plan to be executed. In resource planning we often use capacity profiles, graphical representations of load, offering and resulting utilization, to visualize the situation of a specific work center. Figure 1.11 illustrates such a profile with only the available capacity. In it, you can see that a specific number of hours is available every day within the specified time span of 9 days.

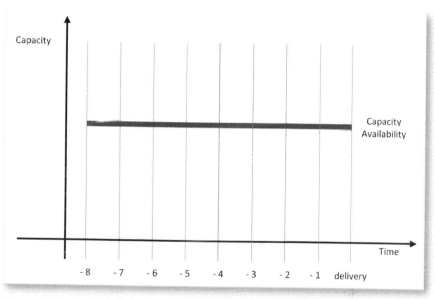

Figure 1.11: Available capacity

Resource availability can be obtained by maintaining the work center record. In discrete and repetitive manufacturing, you can use transactions CR01, CR02 and CR03 to create, change and display the work center and its associated capacities.

In Figure 1.12, you can see an overview of all the capacities associated with a given work center. In the example, we can tell that there are two capacities assigned—machine and person. Therefore, the work center can provide available machine hours and available man hours to carry out a plan.

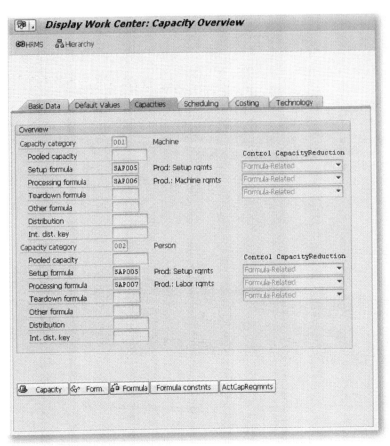

Figure 1.12: Capacities in the work center record

Double-clicking on the category number shows details of any one of the capacities, as shown in Figure 1.13. The screen mainly contains fields for the maintenance of available capacity on the work center. A FACTORY CALENDAR ID can be used so that overall availability is given, taking into account regular workdays and holidays. The available capacity hours for a regular workday are entered into STANDARD AVAILABLE CAPACITY. With start time, end time and the lengths of breaks entered, the system can calculate the available operating time in a workday. A CAPACITY UTILIZA-TION of 90% would reduce that operating time by 10% in order to account for any inefficiencies, regular downtime or other disturbances.

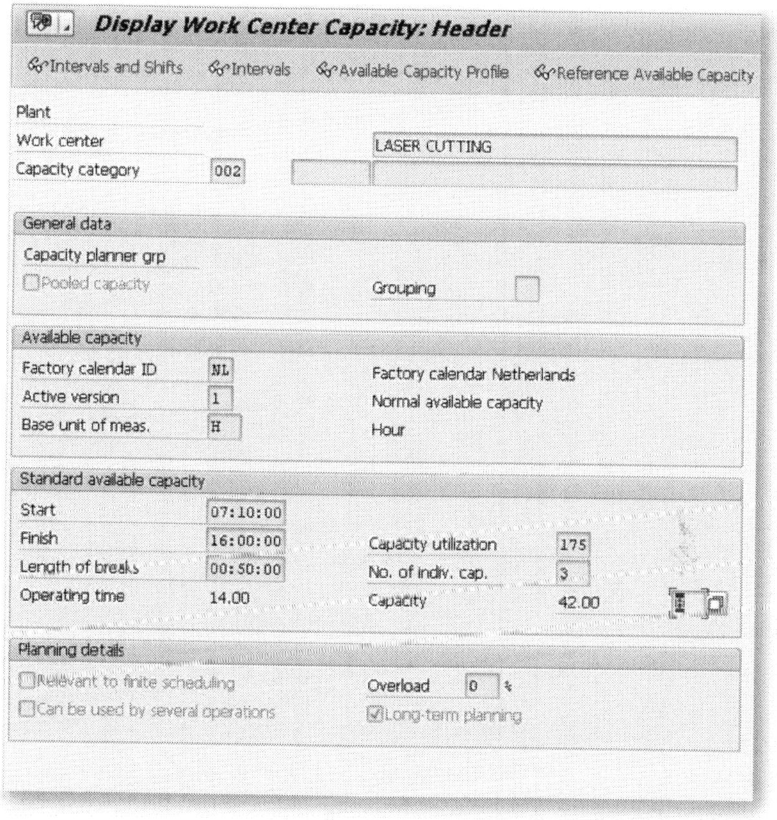

Figure 1.13: Availability data in the capacity header

In our example, we can see that people start working on the laser cutting machine at 7:10am and finish at 4pm, with 50 minutes of break time. The capacity utilization is 175%, therefore the system calculates a total operating time for one person of 14 hours per day. As there are 3 capacities (3 people) assigned to this capacity, we have a total of 42 hours of labor capacity available on this machine every working day.

From the capacity's header screen, you can jump to the more detailed view of a work center capacity's specific shift schedules. Click the INTERVALS AND SHIFTS button and the following screen pops up, as shown in Figure 1.14.

27

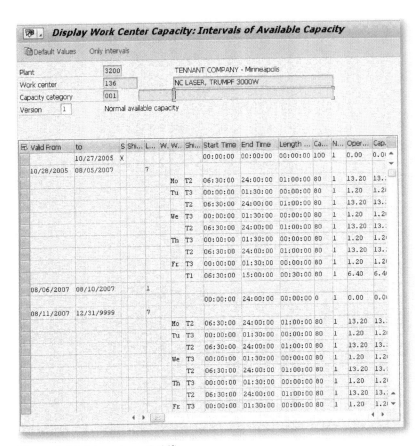

Figure 1.14: Intervals and shifts

Maintaining intervals and shifts gives you the ability to insert work weeks or shifts which differ from the normal working days and times. Should extra demand require an additional shift on an otherwise work-free Saturday, the supplementary work hours can be added here. Also, if your factory closes for a week during summer vacation, you add a work week with zero available hours that is only valid for that time period.

From the individual capacity header view you can also branch into the AVAILABLE CAPACITY PROFILE, as shown in Figure 1.15.

Capacities and their associated available hours can also be directly created, maintained and displayed with transactions CP11, CP12 and CP13.

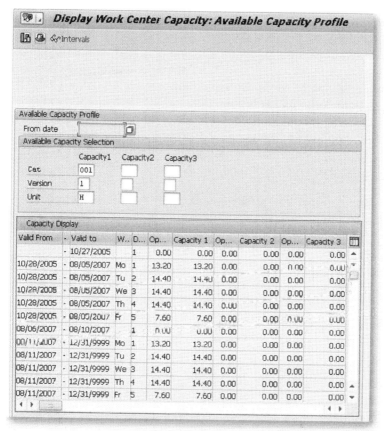

Figure 1.15: Available capacity profile

As I will discuss further in the section about Planning Horizons, available capacity needs to be carefully planned for, based on when and where it is needed, so that it can fulfill an operations plan. Work centers in SAP can be used to accomplish this need in all phases of planning. A statistical or group work center is mostly used in Sales & Operations Planning (SOP) for long-term planning, whereas using regular work centers during medium and short-term planning is the best option. Hierarchies of work centers, with aggregation of available hours, is also possible.

Of course, you can use the same work center throughout all phases. This improves accuracy and guarantees consistency in the planning process for available capacity.

Sequencing orders

Before orders can be distributed on a production line they must be put into some sort of order or sequence because ordinarily you can't run orders on a given work center or production line at the same time. Sequencing orders in a bottleneck work center, in a discrete production environment, is quite complex. Often there are many products with many routings, requiring simultaneous capacity from a busy work center. Additionally, finding the optimum sequence becomes progressively more complicated the more products, jobs and alternatives you have.

Take the example of a single work station with three jobs to sequence. The options are numerous: first job A, then job B and then job C... or job C first, then job A and then...you get the idea. The calculation is 3 factorial (3!—i.e. 3 x 2 x 1 = 6). So, in this example, there are 6 possible sequences to schedule three jobs on one machine. If the number of jobs, however, is increased to 25, then there are 25! possible sequences—that is, 15,511,210,043,330,985,984,000,000 possibilities. If you had this many pennies you could cover the entire surface of the state of Texas...six miles high!

Naturally, if you have more than ten jobs to schedule and there is more than one bottleneck work center, not even the fastest supercomputer can find the optimum sequence. Therefore, instead of racking your brains trying to figure out what additional sequencing tool you need to spend way too much money on, it might be a worthwhile exercise to configure your basic data so that a standard sequence can be developed fairly easily and subsequent rescheduling is organized through a well-thought-out system of exception monitoring—all readily available in standard SAP ERP. You just need to make sure you pick the right strategy and functionality that SAP has pre-configured to fit your company's specific type of manufacturing.

Sequencing jobs on a production line is a bit less involved because jobs on a flow line typically include the routing to make the entire product from start to finish. The objective here is less to level the bottleneck, and more to get the jobs to flow through the stations. Capacity planning for production lines (as opposed to a factory floor with disconnected work stations) requires balancing the operations in the jobs or orders. This is done by making sure that every operation has approximately the same amount of work content. Then, flow line capacity planning builds a sequence according to a *takt*, aligned to customer demand, which flows the jobs over the various alternatives or dedicated production lines.

Figure 1.16 details such sequencing over three production lines and it becomes obvious that capacity planning for discrete production and capacity planning for flow lines must be done differently.

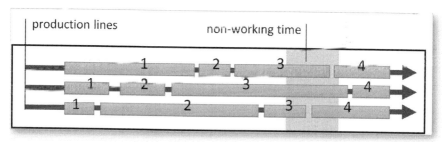

Figure 1.16: Sequencing orders on three production lines

Order sequencing can be done in many different ways. Different schools of thought have led to many variations in how to put jobs into countless sort orders. SAP offers a strategy profile in which, among many other things, a sort order can be defined. Figure 1.17 shows the strategy profile and the field DISPATCH SEQUENCE, from which you can select any one of the different dispatch sequence keys.

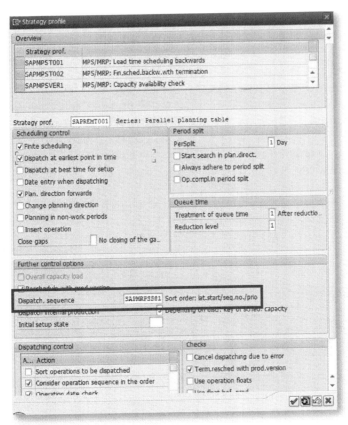

Figure 1.17: Strategy with dispatch sequence

The example shows a dispatch sequence which sorts jobs first by the order's latest start dates, then by a sequence number and finally by a priority given to the order.

Doing a 'pull-down' on the field DISPATCH SEQUENCE gives you a list with all the dispatch sequencing keys, as shown in Figure 1.18.

This allows you, for example, to define a dispatch or order sequence according to optimum setups. In this case, you would maintain materials with 'like' or similar setups with a setup key in the operation of the routing. Then, you make the setup key part of the dispatch sequencing key. When you execute sequencing (dispatching) in capacity management, your orders are sorted so that materials with similar setups are run together.

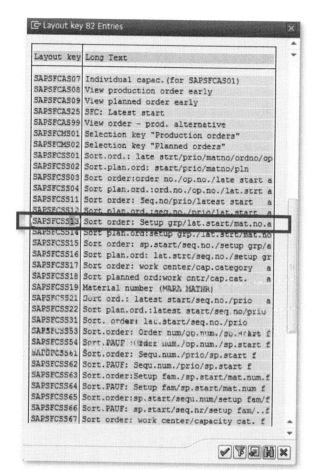

Figure 1.18: Dispatch sequencing keys in customizing

Because you can customize your own dispatch sequencing keys, the options for sorting and sequencing are limitless and you can configure your dispatching and capacity sequencing according to any theory—from FIFO (first-in, first-out) to Drum-Buffer-Rope.

Leveling orders

Once available capacity is known and maintained in the system and a sort order is defined, capacity leveling can distribute or dispatch the sequence over the work centers or production lines within the limits of the available work hours from day to day. This is usually done for a specific time horizon that most of us call the *frozen zone*. In the next section, I will discuss planning horizons and how an operations plan can be developed to become a finite production program within the frozen zone.

Before that happens, it is important to understand that planning is a multi-step procedure. The first task in planning is to create an operations plan at a product group level that doesn't cause infeasible capacity loads on the factory. Once that plan is dis-aggregated onto the individual sellable products, the MRP Run generates supply elements according to policy, to cover planned and actual demand. What's important to note is that the supply program is not checked against available resources but simply set to meet requirements dates.

As Figure 1.19 demonstrates, planned orders generated by the MRP Run (the blue bars on the left) are all stacked up on top of each other in line with their latest delivery date. This causes a very uneven capacity profile. The task of capacity leveling is to distribute or dispatch the orders so that the loads are more even, but more significantly, that they fit within the available capacity.

Figure 1.19: Leveling orders

Imagine an athlete training for the Olympic decathlon. The demand for top performance in ten disciplines is currently due for delivery at the 2024 Olympic Games starting August 6, 2024. If the athlete were to use SAP software to schedule a training regime, he would enter a planned demand date of 8/26/2024 and the MRP Run would generate planned orders with training activities for each of the ten disciplines, all to be finished on August 5. What would also happen is a backward scheduling of these orders where the lead time is subtracted from the end date to determine the start dates for the training program. As the MRP Run does not consider any capacity constraints, the athlete would be under incredible strain in the few weeks before the Games' starting date. Of course, to get into the shape required to perform at the highest level, any sensible human being would distribute the activities better and engage in a more level program. However, more often than not, we don't think about this too much when leveling our production. All too often, this step in capacity management is forgotten or executed outside of SAP, which results in a noisy and infeasible schedule.

Figure 1.20 shows an example of how orders can be leveled within available capacity using transaction CM25.

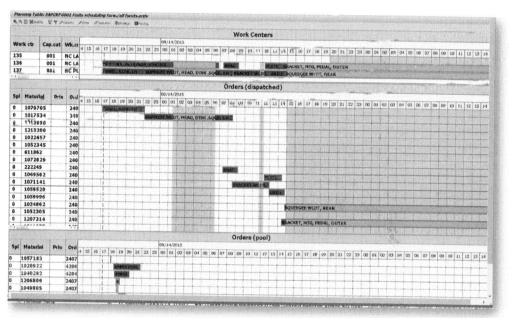

Figure 1.20: Leveling and dispatching with SAP

Pooling, sequencing, leveling and scheduling can all be done in one transaction (for example, CM25) as an automated procedure when the basic data is set up correctly and representative of what is actually happening on your shop floor.

Scheduling orders

The scheduling of orders involves fixing a finite production schedule in time. Many people move production orders around, whereas we recommend executing all the steps previously discussed with planned orders. You can then fix the planned orders, perform a collective material availability check for the components and then collectively convert the entire program into executable production orders. This improves flow, avoids orders waiting to be executed and enables a more optimized utilization of resources.

In Figure 1.21, we can see that scheduled orders, unlike purely sequenced orders, do not stretch over non-working time but are scheduled and fixed within the free available capacity of the work center.

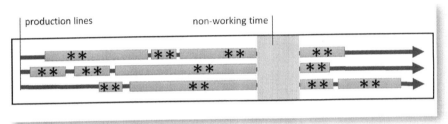

Figure 1.21: Scheduling orders and fixing them

Scheduling of orders can be done for many production types in SAP (discrete scheduling of production orders is not the only option). For example, you can use the tools of repetitive manufacturing when your products are produced according to rates with fairly straightforward and repeatable routings. In this case, you can use transaction MF50 to plan your program and display a graphic similar to CM25. In MF50, rate-based planning allows for much more streamlined and flexible resource scheduling.

Figure 1.22 shows an example of a rate plan for various production lines using MF50 and repetitive manufacturing in the process industry.

Another production type can be found in the automotive industry as well as in many other industries where lean-production supporters plan schedules to a takt or demand-driven mix of orders. Unfortunately, this is a very underutilized function of SAP. It can be lean and effective if used in the right situation. However, although it has been badly documented and poorly promoted, takt-based scheduling of a flow line with SAP's repetitive manufacturing provides tremendous opportunities and at the same time aligns perfectly with modern demands for an agile and lean supply chain.

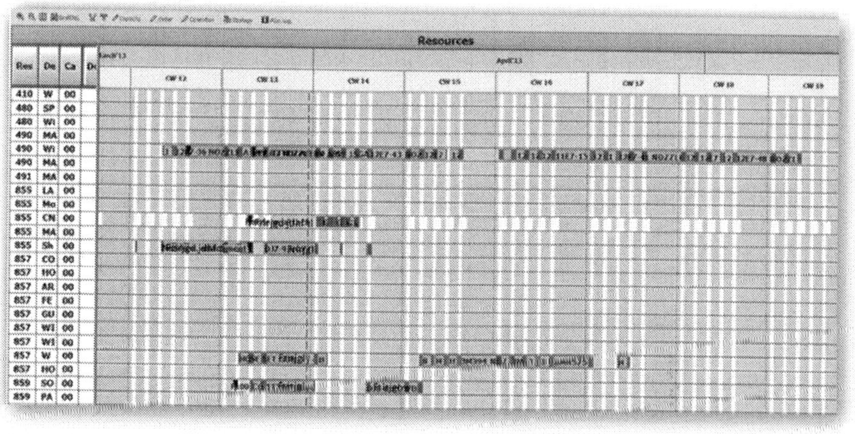

Figure 1.22: Scheduling resources in repetitive process manufacturing

In Figure 1.23, we can see a sequencing schedule based on a takt-based schedule for a flow line with standard SAP transaction LAS2.

Figure 1.23: Scheduling to 80% capacity in sequencing and takt-based scheduling

37

Capacity scheduling represents the last step of the repeatable tasks of capacity management for developing a production program. Once put together and ready to execute, the production program now needs to be evaluated and monitored for peak performance.

Evaluating the capacity situation

Once the capacity situation has been planned for and sequencing, leveling and scheduling have been executed, a production schedule can be moved into the frozen zone and manufacturing can begin. The activities to put the program together usually happen a few days before the actual start of production so that there is time to expedite missing components or raw materials for the execution of an uninterrupted schedule. Of course, the more time taken between fixing and executing the schedule, the more changes and variability in demand and supply can occur.

That is why the capacity situation should be monitored on a constant basis to make sure that all the efforts put into carefully planning a feasible and executable production schedule bears the fruits of your labor. Transaction CM01 is the way to do this. Figure 1.24 shows a weekly breakdown of the capacity situation for any given work center. Capacity requirements, available capacity, the resulting capacity load (utilization as a percentage) and the remaining hours of free available capacity are shown in tabular form. There is also a total given for the period of capacity evaluation.

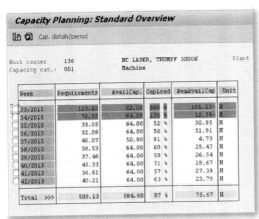

Figure 1.24: Capacity evaluation with transaction CM01

Should there be a problem (overload), as seen in Weeks 33 and 34 in this example, you can drill down into the details of that period. The capacity details screen then lists all the orders—planned, production, process and other order elements that affect capacity requirements (see Figure 1.25).

Capacity Planning: Standard Overview: Details

Order Header Choose field... Download

Plant
Work center   136
Capacity cat. D01

NC LASER, TRUMPF 3000W
Machine

Week	Order	Oper#	Material	Descriptn	Op.	Earl.sta	LtFnExec	Targe	Conf.	MR2	Rem.set		Rem.pxo		Requnts		Stat	Confirm.
Total															38.538	H		
38/2015			1210954	BRACKET WL	0010		09/15/15			016	0.000	H	0.746	H	0.746	H		0000000000
38/2015			383702	ARM, BRUSH	0010		09/16/15			187	0.000	H	0.152	H	0.152	H		0000000000
38/2015			222378	STRAP WLDT	0040		09/17/15			019	0.000	H	0.234	H	0.234	H		0000000000
38/2015			383514	PEDAL, FRO	0010		09/14/15			187	0.000	H	0.297	H	0.297	H		0000000000
38/2015			223637	BLADEHOLDE	0005		09/15/15			016	0.000	H	0.561	H	0.561	H		0000000000
38/2015			222368	RETAINER W	0020		09/18/15			020	0.000	H	0.515	H	0.515	H		0000000000
38/2015			21599	BRACKET, P	0010		09/15/15			187	0.000	H	0.345	H	0.345	H		0000000000
38/2015			1033158	STRAP ASSY	0010		09/17/15			019	0.000	H	0.120	H	0.120	H		0000000000
38/2015			1026610	PEDAL WLDT	0010		09/17/15			187	0.000	H	0.283	H	0.283	H		0000000000
38/2015			1212343	PANEL WLDT	0010		09/17/15			009	0.000	H	1.390	H	1.390	H		0000000000
38/2015			381611	PLATE, PIP	0020		09/17/15			016	0.000	H	0.094	H	0.094	H		0000000000
38/2015			367160	HINGE WLDT	0010		09/14/15			009	0.000	H	0.434	H	0.434	H		0000000000
38/2015			1201094	ARM ASSY,	0010		09/14/15			009	0.000	H	0.556	H	0.556	H		0000000000
38/2015			1212530	WEIGHT, SC	0010		09/14/15			016	0.000	H	0.586	H	0.586	H		0000000000
38/2015			1072421	PLATE, SHI	0010		09/14/15			187	0.000	H	0.069	H	0.069	H		0000000000
38/2015			1033102	STRAP ASSY	0010		09/15/15			019	0.000	H	0.227	H	0.227	H		0000000000
38/2015			81790	ARM, BRUSH	0010		09/15/15			185	0.000	H	0.131	H	0.131	H		0000000000
38/2015			1047166	SCREEN, RA	0010		09/15/15			016	0.120	H	0.314	H	0.314	H		0000000000
38/2015			222240	RETAINER W	0020		09/18/15			154	0.000	H	0.882	H	0.882	H		0000000000
38/2015			1023335	SHAFT ASSY	0010		09/16/13			019	0.000	H	0.408	H	0.408	H		0000000000
38/2015			77592	BRACKET, P	0010		09/15/15			186	0.000	H	0.515	H	0.515	H		0000000000
38/2015			02956	PLATE, FRA	0020		09/15/15			185	0.000	H	0.122	H	0.122	H		0000000000
38/2015			1019636	BRACKET, M	0010		09/16/15			187	0.120	H	0.089	H	0.209	H		0000000000
38/2015			1052345	PLATE WDM	0010		09/18/15			020	0.000	H	1.379	H	1.379	H		0000000000
38/2015			1414474	HINGE, HOU	0010		09/16/15			019	0.000	H	0.525	H	0.525	H		0000000000
38/2015			1201499	BRACKET, S	0010		09/16/15			019	0.000	H	0.350	H	0.350	H		0000000000
38/2015			1200298	STABILIZER	0010		09/17/15			009	0.000	H	1.910	H	1.910	H		0000000000
38/2015			386285	CLAMP WLDT	0010		09/18/15			016	0.000	H	0.176	H	0.176	H		0000000000
38/2015			1052114	SHAFT ASSY	0010		09/16/15			185	0.000	H	0.105	H	0.105	H		0000000000
38/2015			1066260	BRACKET, H	0010		09/14/15			187	0.017	H	4.037	H	4.053	H		0000000000
38/2015			386836	CLAMP WLDT	0010		09/17/15			016	0.000	H	0.150	H	0.150	H		0000000000
38/2015			386286	CLAMP WLDT	0010		09/17/15			016	0.000	H	0.284	H	0.284	H		0000000000
38/2015			368663	ANGLE, MTG	0010		09/16/15			186	0.000	H	0.164	H	0.164	H		0000000000
38/2015			65168	BRACKET WL	0020		09/16/15			016	0.000	H	0.170	H	0.170	H		0000000000
38/2015			1052305	PLATE, MSM	0010		09/18/15			020	0.000	H	1.288	H	1.288	H		0000000000
38/2015			1205043	RING, HUB,	0010		09/18/15			020	0.000	H	0.548	H	0.548	H		0000000000
38/2015			1027294	PLATE WLDT	0010		09/14/15			016	0.000	H	0.159	H	0.159	H		0000000000
38/2015			222368	RETAINER W	0020		09/16/15			184	0.000	H	0.773	H	0.773	H		0000000000
38/2015			1057805	LINK, LIFT	0010		09/17/15			020	0.000	H	0.295	H	0.295	H		0000000000
38/2015			1033158	STRAP ASSY	0010		09/17/15			019	0.000	H	0.120	H	0.120	H		0000000000
38/2015			21597	RETAINER W	0010		09/17/15			009	0.000	H	0.158	H	0.158	H		0000000000
38/2015			1053144	PIN WLDT,	0010		09/15/15			016	0.000	H	0.295	H	0.295	H		0000000000
38/2015			1207018	BAR, END,	0010		09/14/15			016	0.000	H	0.389	H	0.389	H		0000000000
38/2015			1219440	HINGE, GOO	0010		09/15/15			019	0.000	H	0.860	H	0.860	H		0000000000
38/2015			223506	BRACKET, D	0010		09/15/15			016	0.000	H	0.049	H	0.049	H		0000000000
38/2015			1022111	FRAME WLDT	0002		09/14/15			009	0.000	H	0.461	H	0.461	H		0000000000
38/2015			1023833	PLATE WLDT	0010		09/16/15			016	0.000	H	0.625	H	0.625	H		0000000000
38/2015			1060521	BRACKET, M	0010		09/15/15			009	0.000	H	0.367	H	0.367	H		0000000000
38/2015			1046856	PLATE WLDT	0010		09/17/15			009	0.000	H	0.522	H	0.522	H		0000000000
38/2015			1066906	BRACKET, S	0010		09/15/15			016	0.017	H	0.437	H	0.453	H		0000000000
38/2015			84170	BRACKET, R	0010		09/16/15			016	0.120	H	1.640	H	1.760	H		0000000000
38/2015			1024488	PLATE, MTG	0010		09/14/15			016	0.000	H	0.041	H	0.041	H		0000000000
38/2015			1024636	STRAP ASSY	0010		09/15/15			019	0.000	H	0.309	H	0.309	H		0000000000
38/2015			25719	FRAME WLDT	0005		09/16/15			016	0.000	H	0.364	H	0.364	H		0000000000
38/2015			765465	PLATE WLDT	0030		09/14/15			020	0.000	H	0.030	H	0.030	H		0000000000
38/2015			360062	HANDLE, CN	0007		09/15/15			016	0.000	H	0.144	H	0.144	H		0000000000
38/2015			630313	STRAP, SGG	0010		09/14/15			MH3	0.000	H	0.118	H	0.118	H		0000000000
38/2015			1028374	CLAMP WLDT	0010		09/15/15			016	0.000	H	0.451	H	0.451	H		0000000000
38/2015			1038068	NUT, SQ, M	0002		09/17/15			020	0.000	H	0.235	H	0.235	H		0000000000

Figure 1.25: Details of the capacity evaluation

As transaction CM01 is a display transaction only, you cannot manage capacity or move orders from there. You can download a list of the orders causing the overload and resolve the situation with CM25.

This rounds out the capacity management cycle which I will discuss in more detail in The Process of Capacity Management

1.3.2 Planning horizons

SAP software provides excellent planning functions and capabilities. However, before you can use them effectively, you must define the planning horizons as part of an integrated and effective system of operations and resource planning. Sometimes it becomes blatantly obvious that planners or schedulers don't care whether they manage resources (transactions and tasks) in the long, medium or short term.

For example, a scheduler might turn a planned order into a production order several weeks or even months before production of that order starts. Or, the forecast could be done by the MRP Run (and planned orders are subsequently generated) way beyond the short or even medium term.

At this point, I'd like to describe a definition and rule set for planning which I recommend using as a frame of reference if you find it useful.

The graphic in Figure 1.26 summarizes the concept and I would like to emphasize that there are two major rules valid for any planning system:

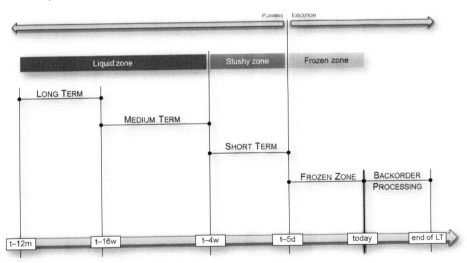

Figure 1.26: Planning horizons

Rule of Planning #1: *'There is a point in time at which planning activities end'.* This point in time is not today! It comes before today, exactly at the point where the frozen zone begins. Once you're in the frozen zone you are working with production orders; production orders are supply elements that we are not planning anymore. We're expediting them, rescheduling them, re-routing operations to different work stations and reacting to exception messages received from the MRP Run when actual results differ from the plan. If you find yourself looking for a tool to automatically re-assign and reschedule within the frozen zone, you either don't have a frozen zone or you're under the wrong assumption that the planning system should not only 'plan' but also fix deviations from the plan. These deviations are due to variability, which can only be buffered but not planned; especially not after it occurs.

Rule of Planning #2: *'Plan your resources in the medium and long term and manage demand. Plan your resources and sequence in the short term, and schedule and manage supply'.* It doesn't make sense to re-shuffle planned orders in the long term. You shouldn't have any planned orders here in the first place. In the long term, you are working in SOP and therefore with a planning hierarchy, monthly demand figures and SOP orders that lead to rough capacity requirements (and not detailed capacity requirements). In SOP, you move the demand so that capacity violations are resolved. In the medium term, you should work with Long-Term Planning (LTP) and its planning scenarios. A planning scenario contains a demand program which you can simulate (with simulated planned orders) for medium-term capacity planning. Here, you should also work with the demand program until you find one that generates simulated planned orders which fit into your available capacity program. That then becomes the demand program (planning scenario) that you activate for the short term. Now you can run MRP on those planned independent requirements and the resulting planned orders can be sequenced, leveled and scheduled in capacity planning. The latter activity deals with 'managing and scheduling supply' whereas the former activities are concerned with 'leveling demand'.

These two rules need to be consistently respected and followed in efforts to build a standardized and integrated planning system which everyone in the organization uses and looks at for continuous improvements. The sales planners enter their forecasts using product groups within a planning hierarchy. SOP Orders, statistical work centers and rough-cut planning profiles provide requirements to analyze the capacity situation for the long term. Should we encounter a problem, we move the entire product group demand into a previous, less capacity-constrained period or fulfill a request for more capital expenditure to increase capacity and meet increasing customer demand.

When the leveled demand is disaggregated from the product group level to the actual product, we then transfer the demand profile into Long-Term Planning (SAP LTP) where we simulate various demand programs and generate simulated supply. Requirements are determined for long lead time items and the procurement process is started if necessary. During Phase 1 of the medium term (12 months to 18 months out in this example) demand changes from the SOP flow in and integrates into the demand programs. In Phase 2 of the medium term, detailed capacity planning is performed with simulated planned orders and the best demand program is found which fits into our available capacity profile.

The activation of the demand program (transfer of planned independent requirements into MRP) represents the move from medium-term to short-term planning. After MRP is run, planned orders are generated which we can sequence, level and schedule within available capacity on the bottleneck work center.

The last planning activity is then to take all leveled and sequenced planned orders of, say, one week and perform a collective material availability check. Now you have ensured that all materials and capacity are available for all the orders to be executed and you are ready to move these orders into the frozen zone. This is done by collectively converting the planned orders into production orders for the next week. From then on—within the frozen zone and in backorder scheduling—all planning will have stopped. Anything that deviates from the plan needs to be adjusted manually. If a work center is down, an alternative work center will have to be found and the sequence in the work order changed manually.

This last point is especially important as we often get asked if this function can be automated. In our opinion, this is an impossible proposition. To actually do this, you would have to build all possible fixes for an exception into the basic data (production versions, alternative bills of material (BOMs) or routings, etc.) and you cannot possibly do that completely. It is much better to have someone who is close to the exceptional situation pick an alternative and just change it in the order.

After all, that is the whole reason why we're comparing 'actuals' to the 'schedule' and the 'plan'.

1.3.3   Capacity management as part of an operations strategy

Every company should have a supply chain strategy. However, even if this strategy exists, it is often vague and lacks the necessary controls, tactics and policies to be executed. A good supply chain strategy is built on a manager's definition of the company's goals. These goals are achieved by implementing policies and guidelines in order to achieve the optimum balance of time, capacity and inventory buffers. This allows for controlled action to buffer unforeseeable variability and variation in demand, process and supply.

Therefore, capacity management is required at the very early stages of planning and becomes an integral part of long-term, medium-term and finite planning. Capacity management becomes essential during execution; without prior, careful evaluation and planning, the operations planning itself is very hard to manage and sometimes overwhelms planners.

When a supply chain can be described as a system where material flows from supplies through manufacturing to customers (as lean practitioners like to describe it in a value steam map), we can look at it as a pressure system where orders are either 'pushed through' according to planned demand, or 'pulled from' according to actual demand.

Figure 1.27 shows a push system that is driven by a forecast pushing a schedule through the manufacturing process. There are three levers — purchasing, production scheduling (capacity planning), and sales — where you have the ability to adjust the flow in order to relieve or increase the pressure that results in inventory or WIP (work in process) buildup.

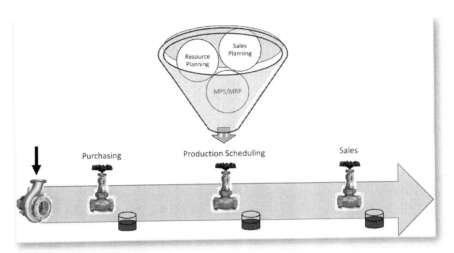

Figure 1.27: A push system

The opposite of a push system is shown in Figure 1.28, where a product is pulled (maybe from customer orders) from the production lines. In a pull system, a time buffer develops and the customer needs to wait until the defined product arrives at their door.

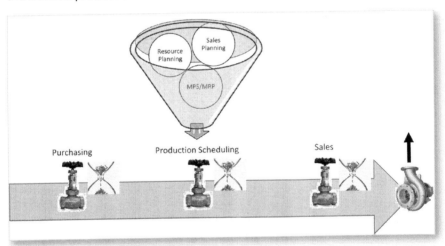

Figure 1.28: A pull system

The key to defining a good supply chain strategy lies in performance of a segmentation so that products can be grouped into different categories or classes. A planning policy can be assigned for each class of products, which determines how the products are planned for. These policies are defined during strategic sessions so that agreed-upon supply chain strategies can be actuated during the planning cycles.

For example, one of the planning policies can be used for make-to-stock (MTS) planning, another can be applied to all products made to order (MTO) and a third one can use an inventory/order interface for an as-semble-to-order (ATO) strategy. Policy setting is an integral part of a system of effective production scheduling and can make a world of a difference to your strategic planning.

Now, when demand disaggregates through the planning hierarchy, pro-duction scheduling can be performed according to the planning policy and assigned to the class of products that a specific material belongs to. As shown in Figure 1.29, the decision to use MTS versus MTO versus ATO is made in production scheduling, depending on the planning policy.

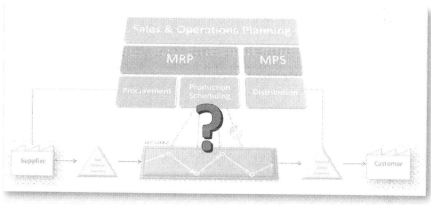

Figure 1.29: Decision on how to schedule

To validate and simulate the decision and effectiveness of a planning policy, you can use demand and supply profiles made available in a graphic from transaction MD04. This forward-looking graphic representa-tion of demand and supply (see Figure 1.30), illustrates the resulting inventory levels of a planning policy which includes an MRP type, lot size procedure, safety stock settings, availability checking rule and a strategy group.

If you change any of these parameters in the material master record, you can rerun MRP and view the resulting forward simulation in this graphic.

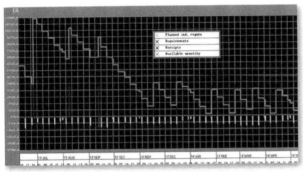

Figure 1.30: Demand and supply profiles in MD04

Therefore, demand and supply profiles provide an excellent means of visualizing the effects of a policy and the execution of a strategy. Demand and supply profiles can be viewed at any level of the cascading information flow in a value stream, as pictured in Figure 1.30: Demand and supply profiles in MD04, and should be part of any discussions about the strategic direction of a manufacturing company.

Let's have a look now at Figure 1.31.

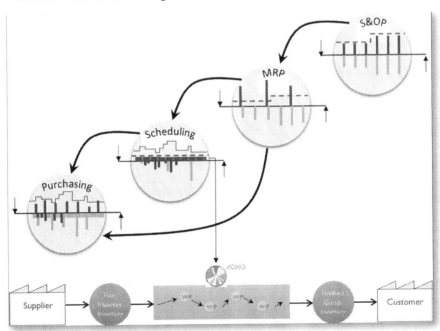

Figure 1.31: Demand and supply profile

A well-thought-out operations strategy uses capacity management as a central component to develop tactics, policies and controls for successful execution of the strategy in order to meet financial goals. Capacity planning can be used to determine a feasible production program that meets demand with relatively short cycle times and high service levels, and without too much inventory.

Without capacity planning an operations plan is infeasible or left to chance and requires constant expediting—a manual process that uses up too much time and too many resources without providing any value.

1.3.4   Different types of capacity control

There are different schools of thought on how you can control and evaluate capacity before releasing a production program. We can either use the traditional approach with finite scheduling or we can introduce flow and perform rate-based and sequenced line balancing. Then there is a rough resource check which is used in SOP, simulative capacity evaluation in long-term planning, and order-specific capacity planning in planned, process and production orders. Finally, in SAP we can also check capacity from a sales order in assembly processing and plan for required capacity in projects for 'engineer to order' manufacturing.

When a planner tries to find out what production program would best fit an anticipated customer demand, some sort of constraint checking has to take place. Planned or actual demand and the resulting resource requirements are checked against available resources in the respective periods. The resulting supply profile should indicate whether the demand can be fulfilled and a feasible production program can be developed.

Most companies use traditional, finite capacity planning to derive such a supply profile. In doing so, every work center indicates its available capacity in hours per period. Then the demand that is to be fulfilled is distributed over the individual work centers using standard cycle times from the routing. In that way, every work center receives a work load for the respective period and can then be evaluated for its utilization.

Another way to check capacity is grounded in the belief that once material can freely flow from one station to the next along the line, there is no constraint on the output of the line. In other words, if the desired demand is met with a feasible throughput rate, then there is enough capacity on the line. A feasible throughput, however, is defined by demonstrated cycle times and work in process on the line. Little's Law (TH = WIP/CT) shows if the feasible throughput is achieved with low/high cycle times and low/high WIP and whether the line 'flows' or staggers along. Once the 'flow' is achieved, capacity is within bounds. In order to meet demand, the line can be sped up or slowed down following the required takt, so that we manufacture exactly what is demanded at the rate to meet the demand exactly.

This second option of capacity management is part of 'takt-based scheduling' in SAP's repetitive manufacturing.

In a similar sense, a certain manufacturing environment might call for rate-based planning with lead time scheduling, a capacity management option for companies that run exactly one product on a continuous line for lengthy periods of time (e.g. a bottling operation). You certainly don't want to compare individual, discrete orders and their requirement for operating times with each individual station's time offering. You don't run out the line after an order for 35,000 bottles is finished, so that you can start the next discrete order for 15,000 bottles to meet demand of 50,000 bottles per week (or 10,000 bottles per day, or 500 bottles per hour, or 8 bottles per minute). You'd rather have the MRP Run generate schedules with throughput rates that deliver the demanded quantity for the period. These run schedules are rate-based and provide us with information about what the utilization of the line will be for a given demand rate in a period. To achieve this, you run lead time scheduling on the run schedules which generates capacity requirement records in rate-based scheduling.

The rough-cut capacity check in SOP uses a statistical work center and rough-cut capacity profiles to give you an idea whether the planned production program covering predicted sales requirements is feasible and can be executed—before you hand it over to the materials planning department.

Long-term planning offers the ability to simulate various production programs. Whichever simulated result offers the best option can then be activated and copied over to operations.

In all of these capacity planning areas, you can pick individual orders—planned, production or process—and run a capacity check on these in an isolated fashion. This makes the most sense in a make-to-order environment, but can also be used for spot checks. A special case of these order-related capacity checks is the assembly process, where an order is generated directly from the sales document so that a specific customer requirement can be covered directly. As the order is being created, an availability check is performed, not only on component availability but also for required resources and capacity.

1.3.5   Gate control in planning

When you run an airport, you must control the gates and check the tickets that were sold earlier. This is no different in production and supply chain planning. You can't just sell thousands of tickets and then let everybody just board the planes. Aircraft are like production lines; they manufacture a service to get passengers to their destinations on time and in the required numbers. And, like a production line, they need to be planned according to their available capacity because they can't be filled beyond their available seats (I know, sometimes airplanes oversell, but that is a policy decision that can be used in production scheduling as well).

However, airlines don't do detailed or finite scheduling months ahead of time. They first roughly distribute their ticket sales over available airplanes and seats and leave some room for variability. The same needs to happen before you do finite capacity scheduling. You first need to see how many tickets (products) you can sell, and distribute this demand roughly within available capacity before you open the floodgates on the production lines. As in the example above, you should also leave some seats (capacity) open for variability and short-term demand (see Figure 1.32).

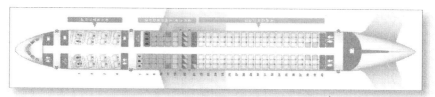

Figure 1.32: Airplane seat reservation

We know from the purchasing department that there are terms and conditions that vendors agree to and decisions for the assignment of purchase requisitions are often based on these. From a materials planning point of view, we don't want to consider these terms and conditions because the materials controller should primarily be concerned with determining optimum supply quantities at optimum receiving dates, rather than worrying about which vendor to pick. This calculated supply is then handed over to the purchasing department so that the buyers can purchase this ideal supply as close as possible to the consumption date and under the best possible terms and conditions. This 'hand-over' represents one of the supply gates. The other one is located in front of the production lines or work centers.

Production lines also have terms of agreement and production lines are sometimes like a vendor. They are the internal suppliers that provide products and components to the planning or sales departments that request these items, based on an actual or planned demand. In a similar sense, the materials planner optimizes supply quantities, dates them and then hands them over to the production scheduler who applies the conditions of the production resources—namely available capacity and resource availability.

As can be seen in Figure 1.33, there is one demand gate and two supply gates in a typical supply chain and gate control is considered an important part of any effective supply chain strategy.

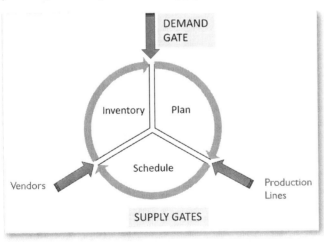

Figure 1.33: Gate control

Without gate control on the supply side, the materials planner is constrained by (costing and manufacturing) lot sizes and other parameters from the shop floor, and is therefore unable to determine the optimum (or most economical) lot size. As this is considered best practice by many, it does not encourage discussion about possible improvements, but rather supports a 'we've-always-done-it-like-that' culture which neither drives positive change nor brings about better performance. A better way to operate is to let the materials planning department think and plan with the optimum lot sizes possible to run the business, and then engage in a healthy discussion with the production scheduler and capacity planner about how to apply real-life constraints from manufacturing to continuously strive towards maximum performance.

1.3.6   A word on utilization

Your utilization rate on the production lines should never exceed 100% for an extended period of time. It shouldn't even get close, because the closer you get to a full utilization (100%), the less you will cope with variability in the process. It is a fact that when capacity utilization approaches 100%, variability multiplies. The urge to do this, however, comes from the standard model of finance which asks for maximum utilization because the business should make as many products or units as possible with the available capacity. This way, overhead costs are spread thinner over more units and make the individual product cheaper.

The standard cost model is great for cost allocation but is terrible for running a factory. Figure 1.34 clearly illustrates that when utilization approaches 100% (1.0), variance and planning difficulty rocket out of control.

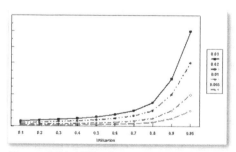

Figure 1.34: Utilization

51

The chart also shows that the more variability you have in the system (the higher the coefficient of variation on the chart), the more critical and unusable high utilization of the production line becomes.

Set the degree of utilization based on the amount of variability you have in the system, and if you want to increase utilization on your lines, reduce variability first.

1.4   Areas where capacity management is used

There are many different areas where capacity planning is not only useful but absolutely essential for the process of production scheduling to work. If you don't sequence and level planned orders within available capacity, you'll get false requirement dates for raw materials and purchased parts. If you don't perform a rough resource check on your production capabilities in sales and operations planning, you might greatly overload or underutilize various periods of manufacturing, MRP and procurement.

1.4.1   Rough-cut resource check in standard SOP and flexible planning

The overwhelming majority of companies using SAP do not perform a rough resource check of the sales plan before it is handed over to MRP. But handing over an unconstrained sales plan to MRP for execution can cause lots of trouble and introduces unnecessary variability right out of the gate

SAP ERP provides all the functions and features needed to perform such a check and subsequently to start the MRP planning process the right way. If you use a statistical work center for capacity offerings and a rough-cut planning profile for the required capacity, you can plan resources with transaction MC82 at product group level, as shown in Figure 1.35.

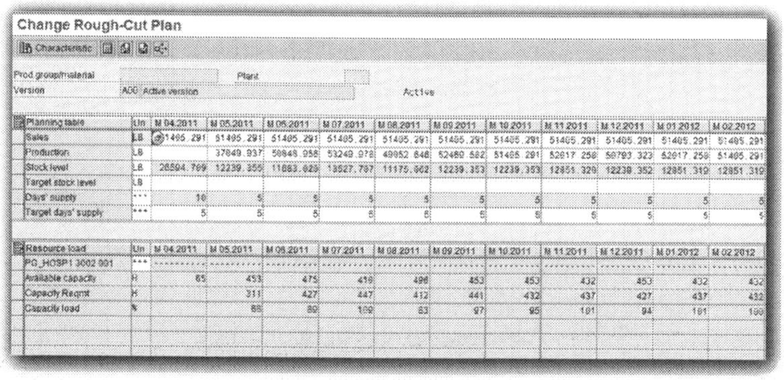

Figure 1.35: Planning for rough-cut capacity in SAP-SOP

Include rough-cut capacity planning into the set of tasks to be performed in your planning horizon scheme and make sure you don't overwhelm your capacity schedulers and production planners with a possible over-load they can't handle.

Effective resource planning is vital to achieve operational targets. With SOP's resource leveling function, you can assess the viability of your targets in terms of the resources required to meet them. This provides the information needed to fine-tune targets and optimize the use of re-sources.

Since sales and operations planning is generally carried out at an early stage in the planning cycle and at an aggregate level, the resource load for work center groups or product families, rather than individual work centers or materials, is of particular interest in this phase of the planning process.

1.4.2 Capacity planning in long-term planning scenarios

Capacity planning in the module LTP (long-term planning—not to be confused with the planning horizon with the same name) allows for the capacity evaluation of detailed, simulative demand programs. Demand can be transferred into LTP from SOP and various versions of supply can then be created to evaluate which version provides the best supply pro-gram to meet demand effectively with the given resource profiles.

In order to identify overloads on certain work centers from the sales plan as early as possible, you can react to these overloads in LTP by re-scheduling planned orders using the capacity planning table in a simulative way. The following evaluations are available in LTP (for the medium term):

▶ work center utilization per period

▶ work center load required for the production of selected materials

▶ detailed display of overloads on the work centers

▶ pegged planned order determination

LTP provides an overview of future plans for production and procurement. Several versions of demand can be checked using a simulated planning run. The planning run as well as the evaluations in long-term planning are separated from the tools in MRP because LTP involves planning in simulation.

Results of LTP can be checked using special evaluations in order to get an early overview of future plans for production and procurement

1.4.3 Capacity checks in sales orders and assembly processing

A specific manufacturing strategy is the process of assemble-to-order, often called finish-to-order or FTO. With this process, any one of the following options is possible when creating a sales order using assembly processing:

▶ planned orders

▶ production orders

▶ process orders

▶ networks

From within these orders you can go directly to the planning table to display the capacity situation and take action if necessary.

The assemble-to-order environment is one in which the product or service is assembled on receipt of the sales order. Key components are planned or stocked in anticipation of the sales order. Receipt of the order initiates assembly of the customized product. Assemble-to-order is useful where a large number of finished products can be built from common components. In the SAP system, assemble-to-order is a special type of make-to-order planning strategy. If you use an assemble-to-order strategy, you can check material and resource availability at the moment the sales order is created. Therefore, the customer can be given reliable delivery dates. Should the complete quantity not be available for delivery because of the capacity situation, the system can tell when the total quantity will be available and whether you can commit a partial quantity.

Continuous feedback between sales and production is another important factor to ensure that customers are provided with reliable due dates in Available-to-promise (ATP). Changes to quantities or dates for production or procurement of components are passed back to the sales order of the finished product, where the committed quantity or confirmation date is also changed. Similarly, changes to quantities or dates in the sales order are passed on to production and/or procurement.

1.4.4 Capacity sequencing, leveling and scheduling in MPS and MRP

The objective of master production scheduling (MPS) is to carefully plan those parts which have considerable influence on the final product. These are, for example, products that represent a high proportion of total sales or that dominate the entire production process because of how they are manufactured.

MPS uses capacity leveling to reconcile the capacity situation before the planning results affect all other BOM levels. Once the master plan for a master schedule item has been created, material requirements planning is initiated.

In MRP, the primary objective is to ensure that the material quantities required by both production and sales are available at the appropriate time. Depending on the strategic direction you take, a secondary objective of MRP can be to make sure capacity is adequately available for the planned orders generated by the MRP Run.

These planned orders can be generated with capacity requirements (if you run lead time scheduling in the MRP Run) and there are functions for capacity evaluation and leveling in the planned order, as shown in the example in Figure 1.36.

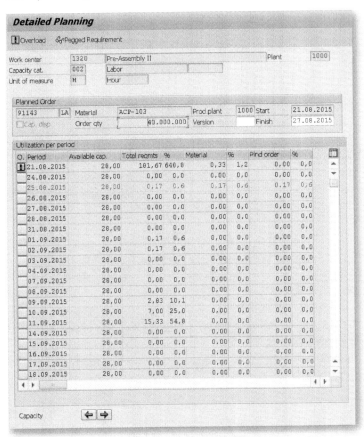

Figure 1.36: Capacity situation in a planned order generated by the MRP Run with lead time scheduling

It is a strategic decision whether or not you want to perform capacity leveling in an individual planned order. Most capacity planning and scheduling systems perform capacity evaluation and leveling on a bottleneck work center for all the operations that cause a load on it.

1.4.5 Finite capacity sequencing and scheduling for discrete orders

Scheduling of discrete orders represents the most common type of SAP capacity planning because most companies using SAP started out with discrete or production orders. When you create a production order, the system automatically carries out lead time scheduling and writes capacity requirement records. Capacity leveling at the production order level is used for detailed planning.

A discrete order is best scheduled using transaction CM21 or CM25 and I will describe the individual steps in much more detail in Chapter 2 of this book.

1.4.6 Capacity sequencing, rate and takt-based scheduling in repetitive manufacturing

Repetitive manufacturing is used for the repeated production of the same product over a long period of time. Repetitive manufacturing uses production versions. You create a run schedule header covering a certain period for a production version of a material. In the material master, you specify task lists and BOM alternatives as well as a production line for a production version. The task lists are generally rate routings.

Capacity leveling is then carried out based on a production line and 'flow' is the determining factor of the capacity situation. Often misunderstood (and therefore not used), repetitive manufacturing provides great functionality to design a takt-based flow line that produces rates for a manufactured product which perfectly fit into the capacity profile of a production line.

The main goal of capacity planning for flow lines is to achieve exact throughput and meet a planned demand with low work in process and short cycle times.

This type of capacity planning differs greatly from discrete scheduling and adheres to both lean and agile principles.

In repetitive manufacturing, you use transaction LAS2 or the central planning table MF50 for capacity sequencing, leveling and scheduling.

1.4.7 Capacity management in the process industries

Process orders are very similar to production orders as they also represent the 'discrete' type. Discrete in this sense, however, is a discrete batch that is manufactured using a recipe instead of a BOM and a routing. The process of capacity planning, sequencing, scheduling and leveling remains the same.

The difference is that in production planning for process industries, capacity leveling functions are used to commit resources instead of work centers. The objective is still to achieve optimal utilization of resources and carry out detailed sequencing.

However, adjusting setup times or performing a setup optimization is not available for capacity leveling in the process industry module (PP-PI). For capacity leveling of process orders, and planned orders that refer to master recipes, campaigns are used to achieve a similar goal.

2 The Process of Capacity Management

Capacity management and its functions for planning, sequencing, leveling and scheduling orders, represent an important step in the chain of events for the lean, agile and efficient provision of a detailed production program. Without capacity planning, we fail to consider reality in our efforts to produce as close as possible to customer demand.

Unfortunately, during most SAP implementations, capacity management is put at the bottom of the list of priorities and, due to budget and time constraints, most often falls through the cracks. Well-meaning attempts to make it work later down the track are often unsuccessful due to the overwhelming mountain of issues that need to be dealt with after go-live.

In this chapter, I want to highlight the significance of capacity management and dive deeper into the individual areas and steps that need to be taken to translate a planned demand and a customer demand into a leveled and noiseless production program.

When managing capacity, we usually go through the following phases: planning for capacity, sequencing orders, leveling orders within the available offering and finally scheduling and fixing the orders into the frozen zone. The capacity situation can be evaluated before, during and after the planning phase. Possible overloads are detected and resolved with specific activities which should be clearly defined and documented. It is of utmost importance that the capacity manager knows which horizon is being evaluated so that appropriate measures can be taken.

It is therefore necessary to detail planning horizons and to identify what needs to be done in each one. Figure 2.1 shows this detail and provides a view of long, medium and short-term planning horizons. It also depicts a frozen zone and backorder horizon where expediting and rescheduling take place.

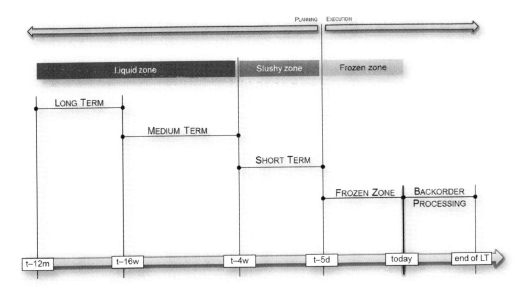

Figure 2.1: Planning horizons

As shown in the figure and detailed in Chapter 1, planning ends where the frozen zone begins and we can arrive at two general rules which streamline the process of capacity management:

Rule of Planning #1: *'There is a point in time at which planning activities end'.*

Rule of Planning #2: *'Plan your resources in the medium and long term, and manage demand. Plan your resources and sequence in the short term, and schedule and manage supply'.*

Keeping these rules in mind throughout the remainder of this book, we can now look at the specific activities performed in capacity planning, sequencing, leveling, scheduling and evaluation.

2.1 Capacity planning

In capacity planning, the user can employ an instrument to plan limited resources at various planning levels. Planning levels refer to various planning horizons within our planning framework. For the long-term planning horizon, we can use rough-cut capacity planning to address aggregated resource requirements and ensure adherence to planned delivery dates on estimated and forecasted dates. For the medium term we can use simulative capacity planning so that a suitable demand program that lies within the available capacity profile can be activated. And finally, we plan detailed capacity in the short term with specific capacity offering profiles on individual work centers and planned orders generated by MRP.

Figure 2.2 shows the various planning tasks taking place in specific planning horizons.

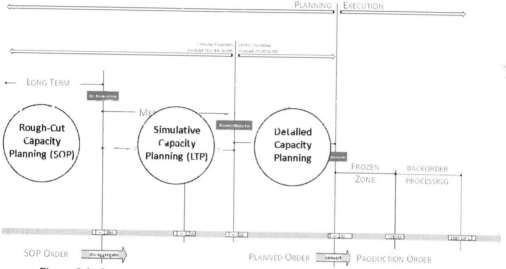

Figure 2.2: Capacity planning

Detail and planning accuracy increases as we move from long-term planning to medium-term to short-term. Moving through the phases we gradually increase accuracy from work center areas to work center groups to the detail of the work center's capacity offering — from months to weeks to days and hours, and from incomplete data to complete resource and availability profiles.

Figure 2.3 illustrates this progression.

Thus, capacity planning is about providing enough available resources to meet demand during the planning progression.

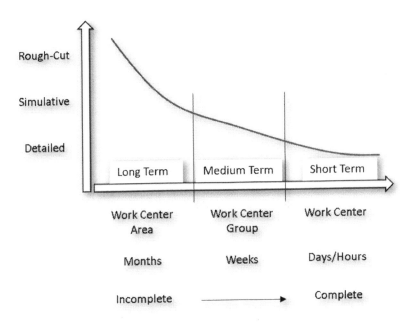

Figure 2.3: Capacity planning levels and detail

2.1.1 Some important planning parameters

In the following sections, I'll discuss the details of some planning parameters which are essential to the planning of a leveled capacity situation. It is important to understand the basic data that supports planning functionality and to operate with a sound setup. This is instrumental for good decision making in long-term, medium-term and short-term planning horizons.

Calculating available capacity

The working hours defined in the work center record are central to planning available capacity. Available working hours are defined for each type of capacity and you can assign as many capacities to a work center as you like. This provides you with the ability to manage various capacity situations. For example, you could make sure that a machine on your shop floor does not exceed its open run time during a standard working week.

Similarly, it is advisable to ensure that workers who are available for 8 hours a day—from Monday to Friday—don't find themselves working late hours and weekends because the order didn't match the availability.

However, labor and machine capacities aren't the only constraints you may have. Warehouse space, oven volume or other space restrictions on a shop floor are just a few examples of the capacities which may have units of measure other than available time. All of them, however, can be set up as a capacity in the work center and can therefore be managed by their constraints.

For each of these capacity categories you can maintain a separate available capacity and assign it to the respective work center.

Furthermore, if a capacity is allocated to several work centers, it is a pooled capacity. For example, the collective available capacity of a human workforce in an area of production can be maintained as a pooled capacity. As such, It must be maintained separately before it is allocated to various work centers.

Once the capacity category is defined, the productive operating time can be calculated, as shown in Figure 2.4.

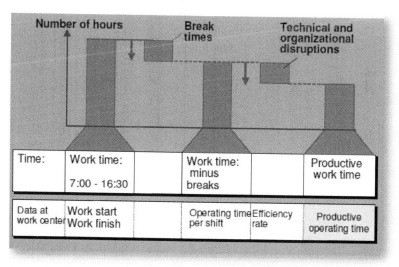

Figure 2.4: Calculation of productive operating time

The basic work time (start of work until end of work) at a work center is reduced by break times and organizational disruptions. Work time minus break times is stored in the work center as the operating (available) time per shift. Technical and organizational disruptions are reflected in the efficiency rate.

Then come the exceptions. Maintaining basic work time as described above, you plan a standard work week and its available hours for production. The factory calendar provides a definition of how many work days in a week. Work start and end times, break times and technical and organizational disruptions define how many hours are available on each of these work days. The factory calendar also contains all the holidays that might come up to ensure, for example, that we do not plan for Thanksgiving Day.

But what happens if we would like to work an extra shift for the next two weeks? Or extend a five-day work week to six, for a certain period in October? For these exceptions, we can use shift sequences. Figure 2.5 provides an example of the definition of a shift sequence. The figure shows that you can define work start and end times that differ from the standard start and end times in a standard work week. Additionally, you can work with shifts and define start and end times specifically for a shift. In a shift sequence, you can become much more detailed, but it is important to understand that a shift sequence—defined by the standard sequence key—is valid for a very specific period of time.

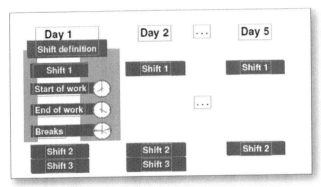

Figure 2.5: Definition of a shift sequence

64

Consequently, shift sequences and shift definitions are used to maintain detailed available capacity for every capacity category, but only by using intervals of available capacity.

Work center	136	NC LASER, TRUMPF 3000W
Capacity category	001	
Version	1	Normal available capacity

Valid From	to	S Shi...	L...	W.W..	Shi...	Start Time	End Time	Length ...	Ca...	N...	Oper...	Cap.
	10/27/2005	X				00:00:00	00:00:00	00:00:00	100	1	0.00	0.0
10/28/2005	08/05/2007		7									
				Mo	T2	06:30:00	24:00:00	01:00:00	80	1	13.20	13.
				Tu	T3	00:00:00	01:30:00	00:00:00	80	1	1.20	1.2
					T2	06:30:00	24:00:00	01:00:00	80	1	13.20	13.
				We	T3	00:00:00	01:30:00	00:00:00	80	1	1.20	1.2
					T2	06:30:00	24:00:00	01:00:00	80	1	13.20	13.
				Th	T3	00:00:00	01:30:00	00:00:00	80	1	1.20	1.2
					T2	06:30:00	24:00:00	01:00:00	80	1	13.30	13.
				Fr	T3	00:00:00	01:30:00	00:00:00	80	1	1.20	1.2
					T1	06:30:00	15:00:00	00:30:00	80	1	6.40	6.4
08/06/2007	08/10/2007		1									
						00:00:00	24:00:00	00:00:00	0	1	0.00	0.0
08/11/2007	12/31/9999		7									
				Mo	T2	00:30:00	24:00:00	01:00:00	80	1	13.20	13.
				Tu	T3	00:00:00	01:30:00	00:00:00	80	1	1.20	1.2
					T2	06:30:00	24:00:00	01:00:00	80	1	13.20	13.
				We	T3	00:00:00	01:30:00	00:00:00	80	1	1.20	1.2
					T2	06:30:00	24:00:00	01:00:00	80	1	13.20	13.
				Th	T3	00:00:00	01:30:00	00:00:00	80	1	1.20	1.2
					T2	06:30:00	24:00:00	01:00:00	80	1	13.20	13.
				Fr	T3	00:00:00	01:30:00	00:00:00	80	1	1.20	1.2

Figure 2.6: Shift sequences in the capacity screens of the work center record

Figure 2.6 contains three intervals: one before the exception, the exception itself (from August 6, 2007 to August 10, 2007) and the interval after the exception, which extends far into the future (until a new exception is maintained).

The concept becomes a bit clearer when we look at standard available capacity and how it can be overwritten by a shift sequence, as shown in Figure 2.7.

65

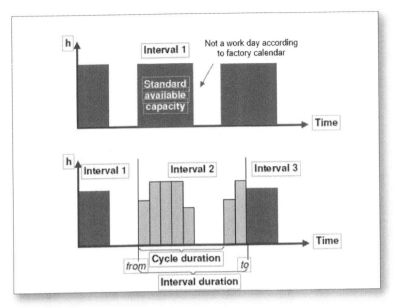

Figure 2.7: Standard available capacity

In the top graph, an interval represents a work week. The standard available capacity is a five-day work week with a set, equal number of hours available on each work day. However, we can now overlap the standard available capacity for a cycle duration, as shown in the lower graph. From the first day in Week 2 (Interval 2) and a cycle reaching the 5th day after Day 1 (Day 6), we provide a different available capacity profile. Day 1 has about 80% of the standard available capacity, whereas Day 5 shows about 70% and Day 9 again 80% of the regular standard capacity.

Note that this 'exceptional' capacity is only valid for the duration of the specified validity range. An interval of available capacity therefore has temporary validity.

Standard value key and formulas

In order to determine the operations' run times in a routing, and to calculate the order's required amount of capacity, formulas and standard value keys from the work center are employed.

The standard value key in the work center determines what specific standard values (setup, labor time, processing time, operating time, etc.)

need to be maintained in a routing operation. By customizing the standard value key, you can also determine whether maintaining a standard value is optional or mandatory. Once the standard values (required through the standard value key) in the routing have been maintained and an order with a specific lot size created, the system is able to calculate the lead time and the required capacity using the formulas which are also maintained in the work center record. Figure 2.8 illustrates the process of calculating scheduling time and required capacity.

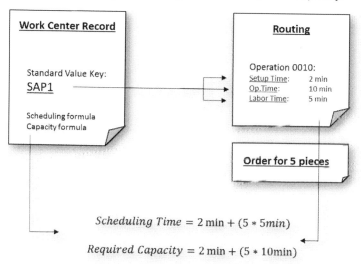

Figure 2.8: Standard value key and scheduling formulas

Standard value keys are an important object for correctly calculating available capacity and therefore need to be selected carefully.

Accumulation of capacity

Available capacity can also be accumulated into higher levels in a work center hierarchy. This enables you to plan capacity availability on an area of the shop floor, an entire plant or even a network within a supply chain. This is particularly useful in the long or medium term of the planning process when you level demand so that in the short term you aren't faced with the impossible task of distributing an exorbitant amount of capacity load onto an available capacity profile that can't even deal with a small part of what is required to fulfill demand.

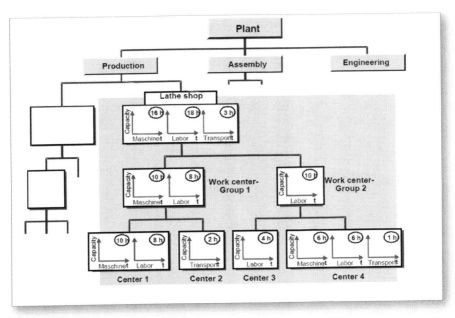

Figure 2.9: Work center hierarchy to accumulate available capacity

As seen in Figure 2.9, available capacity can be accumulated up through a work center hierarchy so that evaluations and planning can occur on aggregated objects.

The descriptions above show that in capacity planning we must maintain and provide available capacity first. Only then can we look at required capacity and determine a utilization rate that lies within a feasible range to achieve flow.

Planning for available capacity and making it available through well-maintained basic data in the work center and material master record are essential in our quest for effective capacity and production scheduling.

In the following sections, I'll discuss how to plan for capacity in the various horizons of a planning system.

A word on utilization

'Utilization' is the actual percentage load of a station compared to its maximum rate. For example: if a station has a maximum capacity (or throughput rate) of 20 parts per hour and we load it with an incoming rate of jobs with 16 parts per hour, then we load the station with a utilization of 80%. Managers with common sense know that cycle times increase exponentially with increasing utilization (especially when you get close to 100%) because of constant variability in supply and demand. It is therefore advisable to plan a utilization of less than 90%. However, over and over again we see that planners try to plan full utilization of the lines and sometimes even plan 110% or even 120%—mostly due to cost pressures from the finance department.

2.1.2 Scheduling levels

Let's add another important thought to the concept of planning horizons and the level of detail we're planning at: scheduling levels.

SAP ERP provides you with the ability to plan, sequence, level and schedule at three different levels. These levels correspond somewhat to the level of detail used in the horizons: long term, medium term and short term. For whatever reason, these scheduling levels are not often used to their full potential, but they provide excellent features to move your plan through the periods and fine-tune it along the way. You can, for example, use different task lists for the long term to those you use for the short term. In addition, you might decide to perform medium and long-term scheduling as period and rate-based, whereas you plan your capacity in the short term to specific dates and hours, even minutes.

This presents some interesting opportunities for your planning efficiency. As most people stick to discrete routings in all planning horizons, there is the possibility to use a rough-cut planning profile for the long term, rate routings in the medium term, and for detailed planning in the short term we can determine exact, planned execution times with a routing or recipe.

If you do this, you're effectively planning rates and periods (such as 20 pieces for August and 5 pieces for Week 25) for when you are too far out for specific, date-based planning and you are planning your order's capacity load to a very specific point in time, with its specific output quantity for the next, let's say, four weeks[1].

Task lists are assigned to a planning horizon in the production version of a material, as shown in Figure 2.10.

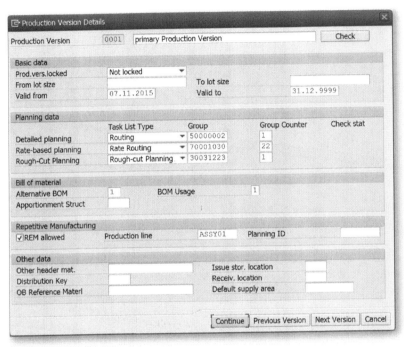

Figure 2.10: Scheduling levels in the production version

In this example, a discrete routing (with a group counter 1 out of routing group 50000002) is assigned to short-term, detailed planning. Interestingly, a rate routing has been assigned to rate-based planning which effectively describes the medium term. You often come across the notion that rate routings are only used in repetitive manufacturing. However,

---

[1] Remember that the short-term planning horizon does not equal the frozen zone. In the short term, you're still planning with planned orders, whereas the frozen zone only contains released production orders.

this is not true because rate routings provide an excellent instrument for period and rate-based planning. They describe a production process with an output rate from the operation (quantity per time) rather than a discrete routing which uses the opposite—the time it takes to produce a lot size (time per quantity). Most people would agree that period and rate-based planning in the medium term more closely reflect the actual business process and allow for better planning results and manageability.

The settings also suggest that for the long term a rough-cut planning profile be used. Rough-cut planning profiles are similar to rate routings, which are meant to plan for rates in periods. But this may be the only similarity these two task lists share.

You define your scheduling levels, and what happens to them, by customizing your planned order scheduling. This customization table has its own transaction code—OPU5. Figure 2.11 shows an example of how the scheduling levels can be set up.

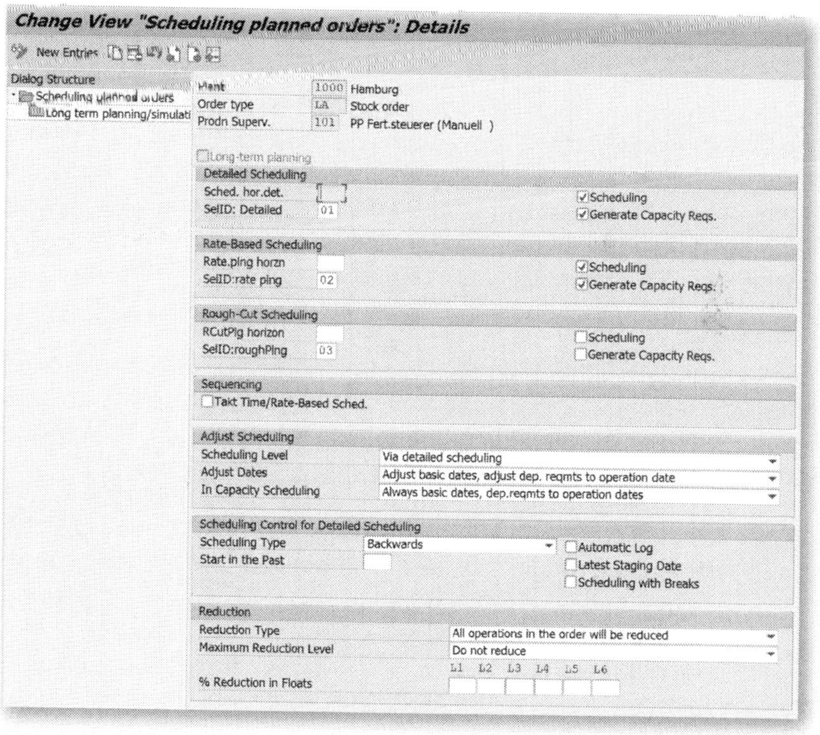

Figure 2.11: Scheduling levels in customizing

71

In this example, planned orders (order type LA) in plant 1000, maintained with production supervisor 101 (production scheduler in the 'work scheduling' screen of the material master), are scheduled and loaded with capacity requirements for the short term (Detailed Scheduling) and the medium term (Rate-Based Scheduling).[2]

No scheduling or capacity records are generated for the long term (rough-cut scheduling).

You can see the results of these choices (settings) after you run the MRP Run with lead time scheduling. In the planned order that is generated, you can see separate tabs for each scheduling level that was planned.

These scheduling records can then be used in the respective planning horizons to plan capacity with the appropriate detail and time frame.

2.1.3 Detailed, time-based and periodic, rate-based presentation of capacity

There often seems to be confusion regarding the presentation of required and available capacity, especially when we look at short-term and long-term situations differently. Add to that the notion that rate-based planning only has its place in repetitive manufacturing, and you're faced with a mess when it comes to implementing effective, three-tiered capacity planning. Let's attempt to organize these thoughts and provide a reference framework.

Generally speaking, I like to associate planning in the long and medium term with periodic, rate-based planning, and in the short term, I believe we must work with detailed, time-based planning, leveling and scheduling of orders.

To better illustrate the two planning methods, let's consider a motorcyclist and how she would plan for trips and other aspects of her hobby.

---

[2] Note that using detailed scheduling for the short term and rate-based scheduling for the medium term is a choice. The decision is made in the production version through the assignment of a rate or discrete routing and the type of planning table we are using (period or date based planning table)

First of all, I'd like to think that motorcycling makes you a better planner. The qualities of a skilled rider can easily be applied to the act of planning demand and supply. Helpful and necessary characteristics such as intuition, foresight, and caution are found in both seasoned bikers and veteran planners alike.

So, when Katy, our motorcyclist, plans ahead, she thinks about how to get the most enjoyment out of her bike. That goal can most likely be achieved by doing as many exciting and memorable trips as possible, within her capacity and the motorbike's performance boundaries. Off she goes and plans for a number of trips over the next four to five years. Katy has heard about the marvelous mountain roads in the French Alps, the long and winding, perfectly sealed highways throughout the Pyrenees, awesome scenery in the Rocky Mountains and nostalgic rides on Route 66. Excitedly, she puts together a list of twenty trips she wants to do over the next five years. That's four trips a year.

Katy lives in Mobile, Alabama and most of these trips (maybe not the one to the Panhandle of Florida) need to be planned very carefully. She needs to consider the time of year that she wants to ride through Colorado, motorcycle rental in Europe for the trips to the Pyrenees and French Alps, and she must watch her budget and distribute the journeys accordingly. Katy intuitively knows that for the long term a detailed plan is overkill. Yes, she'd like to know roughly where she'll go but to plan every hotel and daily routine for a ride in June three years from now is simply not necessary.

So, she decides to put together a periodic, rate-based schedule: 4 trips per year. For every year, she plans her trips as follows:

- ▶ in February, somewhere south of the 25th parallel;
- ▶ a June trip to Europe (France, Portugal, Spain or Switzerland);
- ▶ August in the Rockies, and
- ▶ in October, a shorter ride anywhere where she can expect an Indian Summer in the US.

This would represent a leveled (capacity in budget, available time and mileage) and rate-based plan which puts required and available capacity in periodic buckets to be compared and evaluated.

To relate this to business planning, it becomes clear that periodic, rate-based planning makes a lot of sense when exact delivery and production times are not yet required. The advantage of this is demonstrated in a simplified illustration of the resulting capacity situation from a given demand, as shown in Figure 2.12.

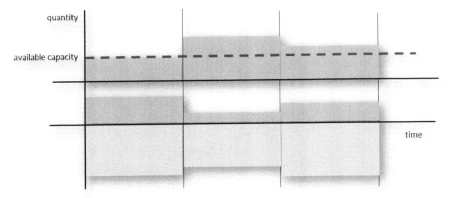

Figure 2.12: Periodic, rate-based visualization of a capacity situation

In this figure, every period has a demand (red), a stock level (green) and a required production rate (blue) to cover the demand while considering the respective stock on hand. In periodic, rate-based planning you look at a period's total quantities and therefore manage a quantity per time period, such as '50,000 pounds per week', 'one A380 per month' or 'four trips per year'. Supply (planned orders) is sometimes calculated by considering stock already available (e.g. we anticipate demand of 50,000 pounds in Week 25 and have 10,000 pounds of stock during that week — so we need to make another 40,000 pounds) and at other times it equals demand (e.g. according to our order book on A380, we need to produce at a rate of one airplane of that type every XX months).

Periodic, rate-based planning negates the need for detailed scheduling, which can be a resource strain and very complex, when dealing with large volumes.

Conversely, in the detailed, time-based planning view of capacity planning, every order has a start and end date. Demand and supply aren't viewed or managed in buckets. Demand is shown at an exact point in time where it needs to be covered and supply is shown in the form of bars, where the beginning of the bar depicts the start of production (or procurement) and the end of the bar represents the completion and delivery of the goods. Figure 2.13 shows an example of demand and (not yet scheduled) supply in detailed planning.

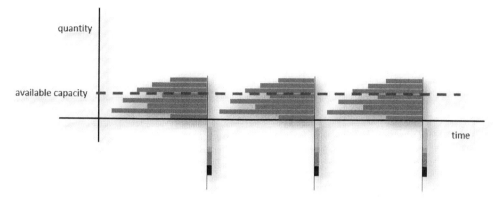

Figure 2.13: Detailed, time-based visualization of a capacity situation

In detailed planning, demand is represented as a total quantity at its due date, at the beginning of the period. The idea is to fulfill the demand just before the beginning of the period so that the demanded quantity can be consumed throughout that period. That is why all the supply is lined up to deliver these demanded quantities at the end of the previous period.

It becomes obvious that we need to do something else before we can actually start fulfilling demand on time and within our capabilities; we need to sequence, level (distribute) and schedule (dispatch) the orders within the available capacity. You might be thinking that performing these tasks for large volumes over long periods of time becomes a bit complex. That's why we recommend using periodic, rate-based planning for the medium and long term but detailed, time-based planning for the short term. After Katy has done her long-term, rate-based trip plan, she needs to set exact times, consult with her friends and make sure she's got all the capacity in place to get on the road.

In the following sections, I'll explore in more detail how you can set yourself up for effective planning in the various scheduling and planning horizons.

2.1.4   Rough-cut capacity planning

Capacity requirement planning for the long term can be done effectively with SAP ERP's 'Standard SOP' or 'Flexible Planning' modules. You might have been advised and tempted to use SAP Advanced Planning and Optimizing (APO), Integrated Business Planning (IBP) or some non-SAP forecasting and planning tool, but chances are that if you are reading this book, your company is running on SAP ERP and 'standard SOP' and 'flexible planning' are at your disposal—for free, with minimum effort to activate them.

Standard SOP uses a product group hierarchy as the planning structure, whereas in flexible planning you can construct your own. For the purpose of this book, and to avoid confusion, we'll stick with standard SOP. However, I'd like to point out that as the name implies, there is much more flexibility and functionality in flexible planning, so that anything we discuss here can be readily adapted and customized to your company's specific requirements.

Long-term planning should always be performed with a periodic, rate-based planning table, as shown in Figure 2.14. This type of visualization allows for long planning horizons and you can see demand, supply, projected inventory levels and the resulting capacity situation all in one view.

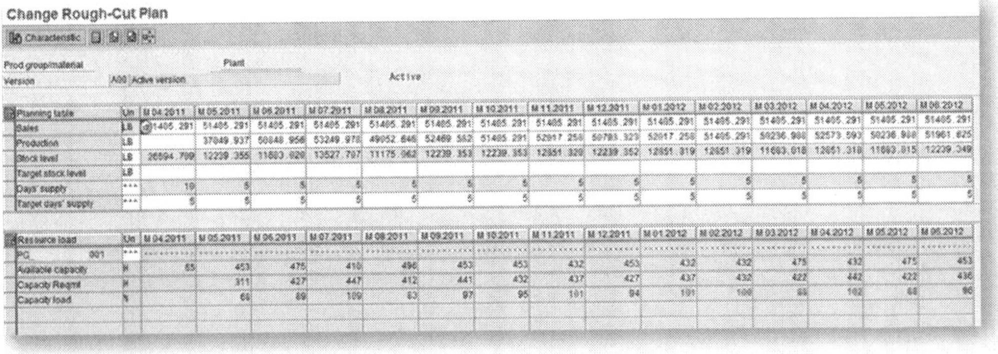

Figure 2.14: Rough-cut capacity planning (in standard SOP) for the long term

This example shows a sales plan distributed over monthly periods and the required monthly production figures were created using a macro. The macro took into account target inventory levels after fulfilling the sales plan and generated SOP orders using a rough-cut planning profile, which acts like a routing to generate required capacity records. Because the macro generated SOP orders, it is now possible to compare a statistical work center's available capacity with the required capacity from the SOP order. The statistical work center can represent a production line, a group of machines or even an entire manufacturing plant, and therefore the plant's capabilities can be cross-checked with a rough production plan which is required to fulfill a forecasted sales plan.

The primary purpose of long-term planning is to check a plant's ability to meet a sales forecast. Rough-cut capacity planning is part of SIROP (Sales, Inventory, Resource and Operations planning) and therefore the sales forecast is evaluated together with an inventory (buffering) strategy and a long-term production program, which should fit into an existing capacity profile. If there is not enough machine or labor capacity available, the planner can make adjustments by either requesting capital investments for more capacity or shifting production overloads into underutilized periods.

2.1.5   Rate-based capacity planning for the medium term

A capacity and demand leveled long-term plan can be handed over to the medium-term planning horizon through the transfer of the figures of a specific demand program (or programs). Ideally, a planner can simulate a number of possible demand programs, so that the one which best fits into a more detailed capacity profile can be selected and activated in the short term.

Opinions differ widely on whether medium-term planning should be done using detailed or rate-based scheduling. Whereas long-term planning most often uses months as the planning periods, a medium-term planner often uses weeks. Most SAP installations I have seen go with Long-Term Planning (LTP) and its simulative planned orders to perform detailed capacity planning.

LTP is a great choice for medium-term capacity planning. Many companies in different manufacturing areas can use transaction MF50 (planning table) for medium-term planning. Contrary to current belief that MF50 can only be used for repetitive manufacturing, it is a great way to simulate various demand programs until the most feasible one is found and can be transferred into operative planning. MF50 has tabular and graphical views of resulting capacity and can be called up either for detailed or rate-based scheduling. It therefore provides an excellent choice for medium-term scheduling but unfortunately is only rarely used for that purpose.

Better yet, we can use the planning table in connection with a planning scenario and simulative planned orders from LTP. There is another transaction code, MFS0, which allows a specific demand program (planning version of planned independent requirements) to be selected via a planning scenario. This enables a specific demand program to be planned, sequenced, leveled and scheduled within its available capacity. Figure 2.15 shows an example of the planning table.

To the left, we can see the products to be planned and their planned quantities per period. Periods might be months, weeks, days or even shifts. For each period, we can see the resulting capacity requirement (in this case in hours). As the work center has a specific capacity availability in the same period, the system is able to calculate the resulting utilization of the work center for that period.

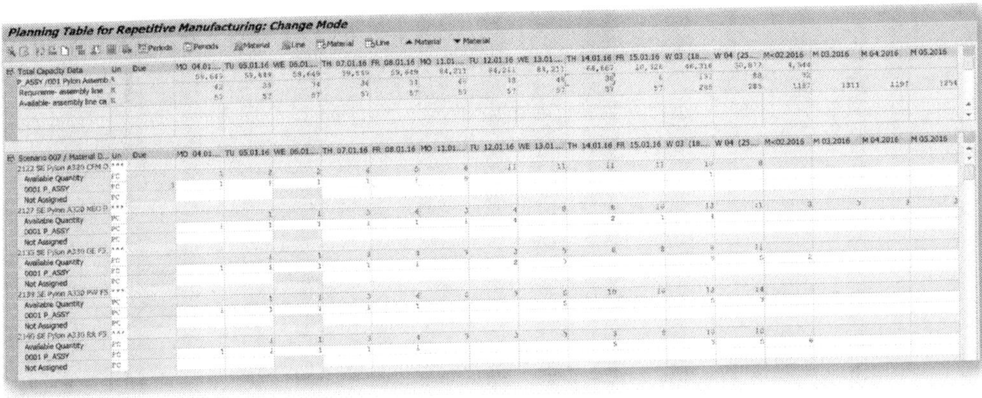

Figure 2.15: Planning table for rate-based, periodic planning

In this example, we can see that 20 pylons are planned for Week 3 in 2016 and 13 pylons are planned for Week 4. The buckets for the months of March, April and May 2016 have not yet been planned. However, we have distributed Weeks 1 and 2 into more granular buckets of daily periods. This was possible using the distribution function in the planning table. Now you can see the specific capacity situations for any given day, week or month, depending on your choice of planning level.

A graphical representation of this situation is also possible. This is shown in Figure 2.16 where every order is represented as a red bar. So far, no order has been scheduled or dispatched and, as a result of rate-based, periodic planning, orders from the same period are scheduled according to their latest end date.

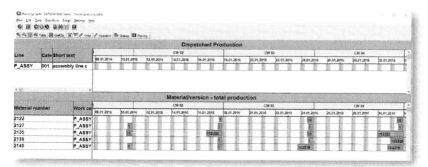

Figure 2.16: Graphical representation of the planning situation in transaction MF50

Unlike the tabular view of the planning table—which is rate-based because it shows total quantities for periods—the graphical view is time-based. Each order 'sits' at a very specific point in time.

Going back to the tabular view, as shown in Figure 2.17, we can distribute quantities from weekly buckets into daily buckets, for example.

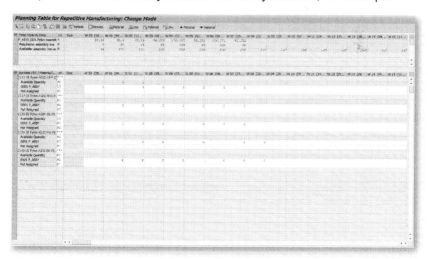

Figure 2.17: Weekly distribution of planned orders

By using the distribution function in the planning table, weekly numbers can be distributed evenly throughout the week into available working days. The result is shown in Figure 2.18.

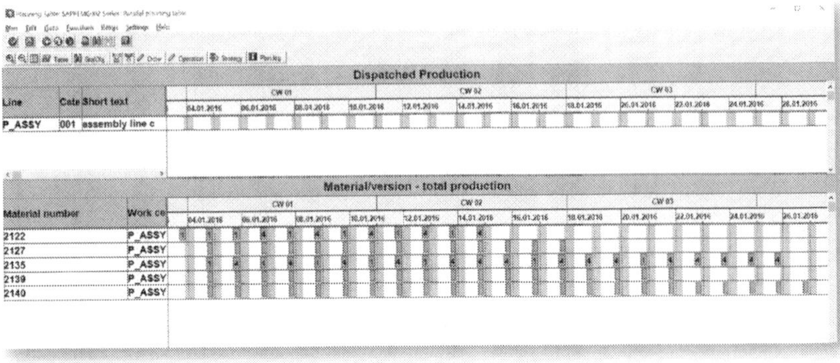

Figure 2.18: Graphical view after distribution to daily rates

In fact, this should be sufficient planning for the medium term. Up to this point, we have looked at demand and supply without focusing on specific start or end dates for the delivery of particular quantities. These precise points in time and quantities become much more important when we move into the short term and start planning with detailed capacity, as will be discussed in the next section.

2.1.6 Detailed capacity planning

Picking up on the previous example of pylon manufacturing, the planned rates from long-term and medium-term capacity planning must now be distributed into a short-term (e.g. a week) production schedule. Because an executable production schedule must have specific start dates, rate-based planning is no longer sufficient[3]. We now have to employ detailed, time-based planning. This is best executed in a graphical planning table where orders are represented as bars—with specific start and end times. Transactions CM21 or CM25 are provided mainly for that purpose. However, you can also stay within the planning table for repetitive manu-

---

[3] As an exception, however, you can use takt-based scheduling (a form of rate-based planning) in repetitive manufacturing, which I'll discuss in Chapter 3 of this book.

facturing[4]. So far, we have been using transaction MFS0 for capacity planning. This is because MFS0 allows the selection of a planning scenario in Long-Term Planning (SAP LTP). Because we are now within the boundaries of short-term planning, we no longer work with simulative orders and can therefore use the 'operative' planning table, by using transaction code MF50.

Figure 2.19 shows the result of dispatching Week 2's orders. As you can see, all these orders are now sequenced and distributed within the available capacity of the work center.

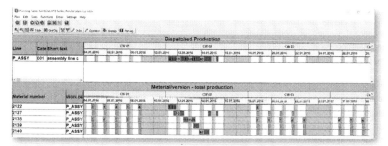

Figure 2.19: Detailed scheduling of 1 week's orders from the pool

In Figure 2.20, we can see the resulting schedule from selecting two weeks' worth of orders and distributing these in sequence starting from Monday of the second week and forward scheduling into Friday of the third week.

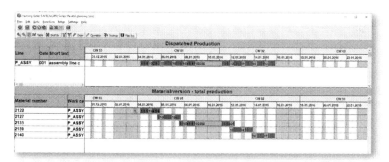

Figure 2.20: Detailed scheduling for two weeks

---

[4] Transaction MF50 is called 'Planning Table for Repetitive Manufacturing'. This is at times a bit confusing because discrete production orders and planned orders with the order type LA are also suitable for planning with MF50.

Detailed scheduling of orders can also be executed in transactions CM25 or CM29 (which both are essentially allowing for the same functions to be carried out), the graphical planning table for discrete orders. There are a wide variety of profiles available in these transactions. Using profiles, you can customize the layout, time periods, even color codes and much more.

No matter what transactions are used for detailed capacity planning, they should be used for planned orders, not production orders. This is because detailed scheduling happens in the short-term planning horizon and not in the 'frozen zone'. The transition from short-term planning into the frozen zone happens after checking collective material availability on scheduled planned orders and then performing collective conversion into released production orders.

Any other process flow could result in production orders blocking valuable available capacity on work centers because the order can't be completed while waiting for missing parts.

Figure 2.21 shows an example of detailed capacity planning with CM25. Orders from the pool (lower part of the screen) can be distributed or dispatched to the work centers within the work center's available capacity (upper part of the screen).

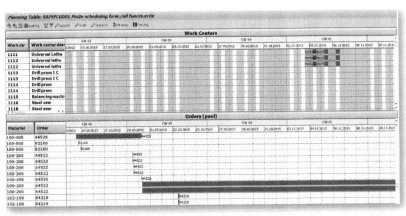

Figure 2.21: Capacity planning screen in transaction CM25

I've now explained what needs to be set up for capacity planning. In the next section, I will address the options for how you can sequence the orders before dispatching them on the line.

2.2 Sequencing of orders

As we know, the MRP Run generates supply to cover planned or actual demand. In the case of internal procurement (we produce what is needed in our own plant), the procurement proposals are planned orders. If the MRP Run is started with lead time scheduling, the routing (and its operations and standard values) is used to determine production start and end dates, and required capacity is calculated. Because MRP is not responsible for the capacity situation on the work centers, it simply places all planned orders in the timeline according to their latest possible end dates (and times).

The bottom of the graphic in Figure 2.22 illustrates this. Therefore, if we want to consider available capacity and distribute the planned orders so that they can be executed within It, we have to first sort and sequence the orders according to some sort of priority. Sorting and sequencing must happen before we can distribute the orders onto the work center within available capacity (finite scheduling).

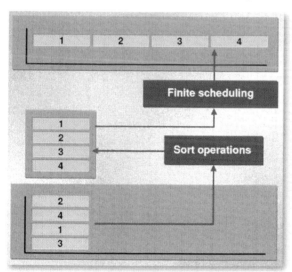

Figure 2.22: Sequencing orders

Of course, you can sequence planned orders manually in the planning table with a simple drag and drop. However, if you want to automate the process, you must identify a sequencing key in the strategy profile, as shown in Figure 2.23. In this example, we are using a dispatch sequence which first sorts the orders according to a Setup Group Key, and then according to a setup Key.

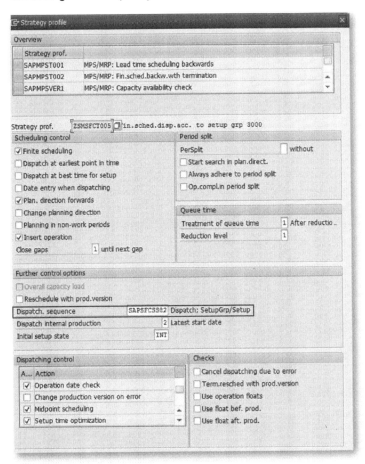

Figure 2.23: Sequencing key

The dispatch sequence key can be customized and provides you with a vast array of options to comply with all sorts of policies and strategies such as heijunka, FIFO, setup optimization or Drum-Buffer-Rope. Figure 2.24 shows some of the pre-configured dispatch sequence keys you could use to sort orders and operations.

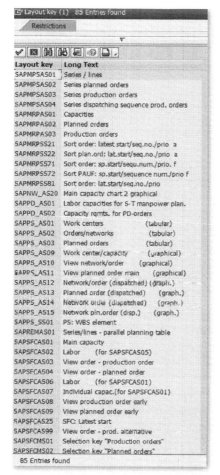

Figure 2.24: Pre-configured dispatch sequence keys

In the following section, I will describe some of the sequencing policies and how you can use them in SAP ERP.

2.2.1 Heijunka sequencing

Heijunka is a term mainly associated with the Toyota Production Process and with lean production philosophies. It is used by lean practitioners and allows for even distribution according to the EPEI (Every Part Every Interval) principle. EPEI suggests that you have every part on the schedule, every period—i.e. a small amount of each part is produced every shift, every day, every week or every month, depending on how your scheduling periods are defined. Heijunka then distributes orders evenly over a specific period and sequences them according to the principle of equal distribution.

Heijunka is a Japanese word meaning 'leveling'. Leveling can be done by volume or by product. If, for example, a family of products that uses the same production process has demand that varies between 1,000 and 2,000 units, then it might seem a good idea to produce the exact amount that was ordered by the customer. However, it has been proven that doing this introduces a very high level of noise into a system which is already exposed to variability. Distributing the demand in equal, average quantities over a certain period of time provides a much more reliable supply to fulfill fluctuating order quantities.

On the other hand, many value streams produce a mix of products and, therefore, decisions have to be made in terms of product combination and sequence. It is here that economic order quantities are discussed and are dominated by changeover times and the inventory this requires. Toyota's approach has resulted in a different situation whereby it has reduced the time and cost of changeovers so that smaller and smaller batches are not prohibitive, and lost production time and quality costs are not significant. This means that the demand for products could be leveled for upstream processes and therefore lead time and total inventories can be reduced along the entire value stream.

Figure 2.25 shows the progression of first leveling volume and then equalizing the mix of parts (green, yellow and red).

The whole point of leveling mix and volume is to protect and 'calm' a production schedule; the aim being to buffer and fulfill ever-changing demand. To do so, we must move away from producing exact demand at the exact time when it is demanded. Instead, we distribute demand evenly over a specific period and we must therefore hold on to some inventory to fulfill the demand during that period.

So, what's on the line this week is NOT for this week's demand, it's for next week's.

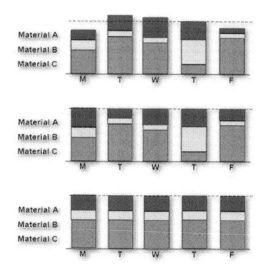

Figure 2.25: Leveling mix and volume

That kind of thinking often requires breaking down existing mental models, which is hard to do. More often than not, heijunka seems to be the right choice but it fails when it comes to execution.

Figure 2.26 illustrates how you can apply heijunka and evenly distribute the demand for three parts into a production schedule for semi-finished and finished goods.

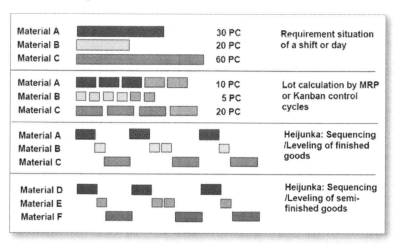

Figure 2.26: Even distribution of demand for three parts over specific periods

Heijunka can easily be configured into SAP ERP. If you run in a repetitive manufacturing environment, the option is already pre-configured and ready to use (you must run on ECC 6.0 Enhancement Pack 3 to have the option available). There is an option in takt-based scheduling to plan according to the heijunka principle of equal distribution, as seen in Figure 2.27 (more about takt-based scheduling and heijunka distribution in Chapter 3). The other choices include FIFO (which I'll discuss in Section 2.2.4), manual dispatching or the creation of a user exit, which give you many more possibilities for scheduling.

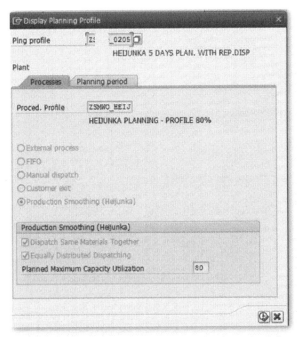

Figure 2.27: Picking a procedure profile for scheduling and distribution of orders in repetitive manufacturing

If you work with discrete orders (as opposed to 'run schedules' or repetitive orders), you can configure a dispatch sequence that distributes your discrete orders according to heijunka, as illustrated in Figure 2.28.

As you can see in Figure 2.29, the orders from the pool and its operation have been distributed equally within the available capacity of the work center. The equal distribution was driven by a dispatch sequencing key maintained in customizing.

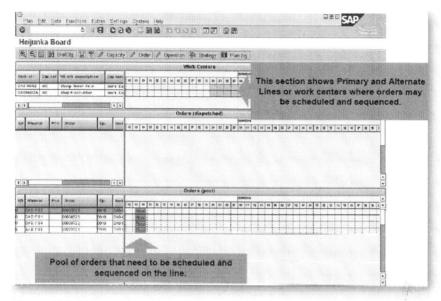

Figure 2.28: Discrete orders waiting to be distributed and dispatched

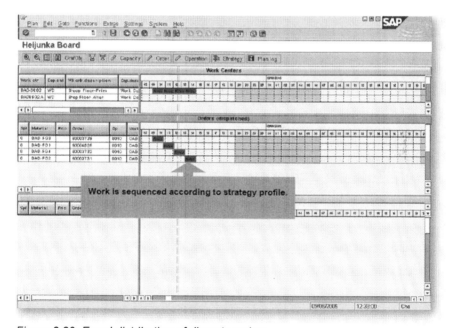

Figure 2.29: Equal distribution of discrete orders.

Heijunka provides an excellent opportunity to protect a production program from variability in demand and it reduces the variability in supply. In most cases, implementing heijunka isn't difficult. Often, the old way of 'order-based' thinking stands in the way of its success.

2.2.2 Setup optimization

When complex setup or lengthy machine changes affect your manufacturing environment, a sequence that optimizes the time it takes to switch from one production lot to another might just be the thing to use. SAP ERP provides you with a setup group category and a setup group key which you can use to do setup optimization.

Setup optimization is carried out using a specific setting in the strategy profile, as displayed in Figure 2.30. A number of prerequisites must be fulfilled (I'll discuss these in the following section) but you might have to check 'Setup time optimization' for it to work.

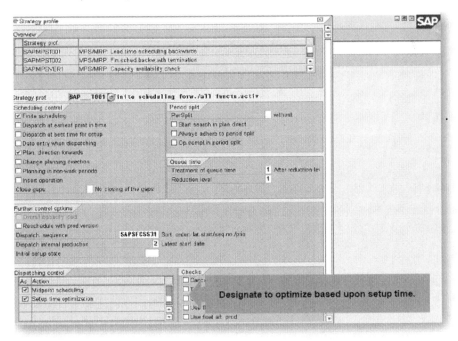

Figure 2.30: Switching on setup time optimization in the strategy profile

An interesting and little-known fact is that you can color code order bars in the graphical planning table. Figure 2.31 shows various colors designating status, timing and other order characteristics. For example, you could identify the setup time and teardown portion of an order using the color blue.

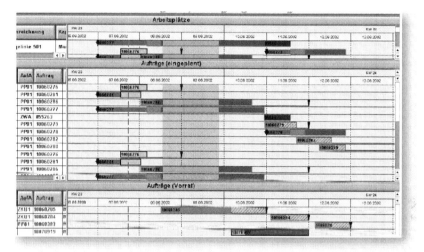

Figure 2.31: Color coding of orders in the graphical planning table

Using color coding, orders with the same or similar setup can be sequenced together and dispatched on designated production lines or work centers, as shown in Figure 2.32.

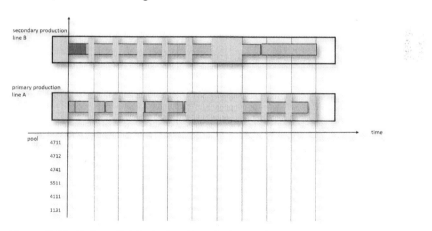

Figure 2.32: Orders distributed on two designated production lines according to similar setups

91

Figure 2.33 provides another example of color-coded orders in the graphical planning table.

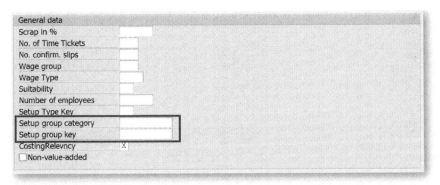

Figure 2.33: Color-coded operations in the graphical planning table CM25

For setup optimization sequencing to work, you must use a setup group category and a setup group key in the operation that is to be dispatched. Setup group key and setup group category are configured in customizing and can be allocated to a product in an operation of the product's routing, as seen in Figure 2.34.

General data	
Scrap in %	
No. of Time Tickets	
No. confirm. slips	
Wage group	
Wage Type	
Suitability	
Number of employees	
Setup Type Key	
Setup group category	
Setup group key	
CostingRelevncy	X
☐ Non-value-added	

Figure 2.34: Setup group category and setup group key in the detailed screen of an operation

Once the setup group key and setup group category have been config-ured and customized to your specific needs, a layout key can be con-structed so that the dispatch sequence is executed according to these keys and categories. Figure 2.35 demonstrates how setup group catego-ry, setup group key and the latest start date are employed in the dispatch sequence SAPSFCSS82.

Field Selection for Display Fields

Sequence/Heading   Structures   Subview

Layout key   [SAPSFCSS82] Dispatch: SetupGrp/Setup

Long Fld Label	Short Descript.	Table Name	Field Name	Offset	Outp...	
Setup group category	Order operation	AFVGD	RFGRP	0	10	
Setup group key	Order operation	AFVGD	RFSCH	11	10	
Latest start date	Order operation	AFVGD	SSAVD	22	10	
Account assignment	Order operation	AFVGD	NETZKONT	0	1	
Act./Operation UoM	Order operation	AFVGD	MEINH	0	3	
Activity Type	Order operation	AFVGD	LARNT	0	6	
Activity Type	Order operation	AFVGD	LAR06	0	6	
Activity Type	Order operation	AFVGD	LAR05	0	6	
Activity Type	Order operation	AFVGD	LAR04	0	6	
Activity Type	Order operation	AFVGD	LAR03	0	6	
Activity Type	Order operation	AFVGD	LAR02	0	6	
Activity Type	Order operation	AFVGD	LAR01	0	6	
Actual finish	Order operation	AFVGD	ICAVD	0	10	
Actual finish (date)	Order operation	AFVGD	IEDD	0	10	
Actual finish (date)	Order operation	AFVGD	IEBD	0	10	
Actual finish (time)	Order operation	AFVGD	IEDZ	0	8	
Actual start (date)	Order operation	AFVGD	ISDD	0	10	
Actual start (time)	Order operation	AFVGD	ISDZ	0	8	

Figure 2.35: Sequence layout key configuration in customizing transaction CY39

There is also the option of using a setup matrix when the setup of an operation depends on the state of the work center. The state of the work center often depends on the product or operation that was previously run on that same work center. In food processing, for example, you have to be careful with allergens; the time it takes to clean between product runs depends on the type of allergen which was run before and the one that runs after.

If you use the setup matrix, as shown in Figure 2.36, the system does not consider the setup times in the operation's standard values, but ra-ther calculates the standard values from the setup matrix.

Change View "Setup Matrix": Overview

New Entries

Plnt	Pred.group	PreSubgrp	Succ.group	SuccSubgrp	Standard Val...	Unit	SNo
1000	1	*	1	*	100	MIN	
1000	1	10	1	10	1	MIN	1
1000	1	10	1	20	10	MIN	1
1000	1	10	1	30	15	MIN	1
1000	1	10	1	40	20	MIN	1
1000	1	10	1	50	25	MIN	1
1000	1	20	1	10	30	MIN	1
1000	1	20	1	20	1	MIN	1
1000	1	20	1	30	10	MIN	1
1000	1	20	1	40	15	MIN	1
1000	1	20	1	50	20	MIN	1
1000	1	30	1	10	30	MIN	1
1000	1	30	1	20	25	MIN	1
1000	1	30	1	30	1	MIN	1
1000	1	30	1	40	10	MIN	1
1000	1	30	1	50	15	MIN	1
1000	1	40	1	10	30	MIN	1
1000	1	40	1	20	25	MIN	1
1000	1	40	1	30	15	MIN	1
1000	1	40	1	40	1	MIN	1
1000	1	40	1	50	10	MIN	1

Figure 2.36: Setup matrix using setup group keys and standard values

In the setup matrix, the outcome of the setup (or cleaning time) is determined as follows:

▶ The setup state of a work center is defined in terms of the setup group category and the setup group key of the operation that is processed at the work center.

▶ A setup transition is an arrangement of two operations—a predecessor and a successor—that are processed sequentially at the work center.

▶ A setup standard value for the successor is assigned to the setup transition.

A setup matrix can also be used with wild cards. You do not have to define each setup transition explicitly. You can define generic setup transitions in the setup matrix using a wild card (*), which is entered in a setup transition instead of a setup group. However, the wild card (*) only replaces the setup groups that you also use in the setup matrix specifically to define setup transitions, and not all setup groups that you define for the location.

2.2.3 The product wheel

The product wheel is a concept mostly used in the process industry. However, it is by no means limited to this and has also been used effectively in discrete manufacturing. It is a sequencing concept which allows for standardized, noise-reduced production of fast and slow moving products made to stock and made to order.

If your company is a process manufacturer, you most likely mix, blend, cure or otherwise process your products on a production line. One of the characteristics of processed products is that they can't be disassembled. You can usually 'unscrew' an automobile, for example, and put the components back into inventory (even though this is not 100% true, it is an approximate way of differentiating between process and discrete manufacturing).

In process manufacturing, you might also have by-products and co-products (unfinished yield that can be re-introduced into the process) and you often can't predict exactly what will come out of the process. So, you have to work with ranges (of specifications) and chemical formulas. This is all provided with recipes and process orders in PP-PI. As 'lean manufacturing' comes primarily from the automotive industry, process manufacturers have always asked whether they can also reduce waste. Why not? You can't introduce 'one piece flow', but that's not the only lean principle. Why not heijunka level a production program or make every product every interval (EPEI)?

Peter L. King has written a book 'Lean for the Process Industries. Dealing with Complexity' (King, 2009), which beautifully translates all the 'automotive lean principles' into process manufacturing. One of the most interesting ideas is the 'product wheel'. It represents heijunka for processed products. Products wheels allow you to simultaneously schedule, capacity level and sequence your production program. It is a mixed model scheduling concept which allows you to automatically fill a processing line to its capacity in a setup-optimized sequence, ensuring that the smallest possible lot size is processed as many times as possible within a planning cycle.

In this concept, a circle represents the lengths of the planning cycle, as shown in Figure 2.37. Each segment is a batch size (the lengths in time for production) of a specific product and the gap in-between represents the time it takes to set up, clean or prep the line for the next product. Note that there are segments for MTO (A, B, C, D or E) and segments for MTS (1 and 2). The MTS segments are planned based on a forecast, whereas the MTO segments are reserved time / capacity which can be filled by customer requests when fulfilled to order.

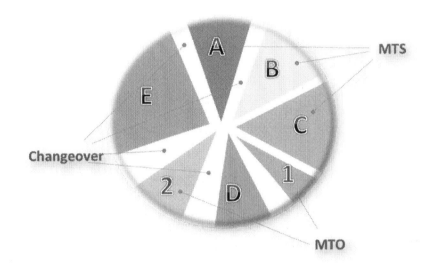

Figure 2.37: Product wheel scheduling—MTS / MTO mix

A planner first identifies how much time is available during a planning cycle to get all the way around the wheel. If that timespan is one week, we simply sequence the total forecasted quantity for all products on that line and for the week around the wheel. If, for example, we get 2/3 of the way around the wheel, then there is 1/3 available for MTO capacity and setup time. You might use the extra time and capacity for more setups or changeovers (to manufacture in smaller batches) instead of producing larger batches which result in waste from overproduction.

The way you configure the product wheel philosophy into SAP ERP is mainly driven by the setup group key and the setup group category in conjunction with a dispatch sequence, as described in the previous section.

Like other sequencing methods, the product wheel can be executed using transaction CM25. An example can be seen in Figure 2.38.

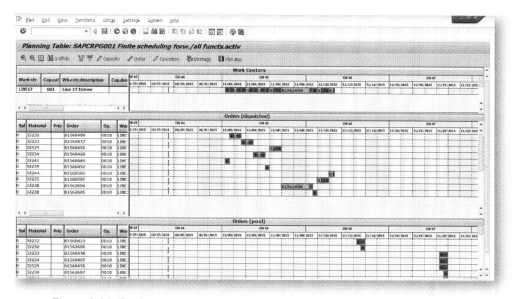

Figure 2.38: Product wheel sequencing in CM25

As discussed, product wheel sequencing is not limited to use in the process industry. There are plenty of discrete manufacturers using this method in order to benefit from a uniform, leveled and periodic production schedule.

2.2.4　First-in, First-out

Sequencing in SAP ERP can also simply be done according to a priority of planned order dates. The FIFO method is when your dispatch sequence sorts the orders by their start or end dates. The easiest way to sequence according to FIFO is by using the planned orders' sequentially generated order numbers, which is especially suited to sorting orders in an MTO or ATO environment.

In this situation, planned, process or production orders are often generated directly from the sales order and must then be executed according to the order in which the customer requests came in.

2.3   Capacity leveling

After orders have been sequenced and put into an order of execution, capacity leveling can take place. The orders are dispatched within the available capacity of one or more work stations or production lines. In fact, it is a specific operation for the order that is being dispatched and the dispatching takes place on the bottleneck work center. As discussed previously, a bottleneck is the work center with the highest utilization — the busiest one. If orders are spread out over the busiest work center, it is then most likely that all the other operations can be executed on their assigned work centers without any problems. However, for a multitude of reasons, another work center could become the bottleneck after dispatching and therefore the whole process of leveling becomes progressively more difficult and cumbersome.

In standard SAP ERP, there are two primary transactions to handle this situation. CM25 for leveling, and transaction CM01 to evaluate the capacity situation and find possible overloads and the bottleneck (I will explore capacity evaluation in more detail on page 103, Section 2.5). Therefore, as you start leveling you have to go back and forth between these transactions so that you can evaluate the new situation in CM01 and subsequently level the new bottleneck with CM25.

A valid alternative to this elaborate process is the SAP Add-on Tool 'Capacity Requirements Monitor' (CRP Monitor). As shown in the screenshot in Figure 2.39, the CRP Monitor allows you to view a 'heat map'. In it, a red light indicates a capacity overload and double-clicking on the red light brings up all the orders which have caused the overload. From here, you can go into the leveling functions of CM25 without ever leaving the monitor. And once leveling of the bottleneck is done, you simply go back to the heat map so that you can level another bottleneck that might have appeared due to leveling.

The Capacity Requirements Monitor, as well as the other SAP Add-On Tools, are available at an additional cost from SAP Consulting in Germany or bigbyte software systems in the US.

Besides leveling orders within the available capacity of the bottleneck work center, you also have the option to adjust the available capacity by increasing the standard available capacity for the relevant capacity category or to increase the available capacity by inserting an interval of available capacity.

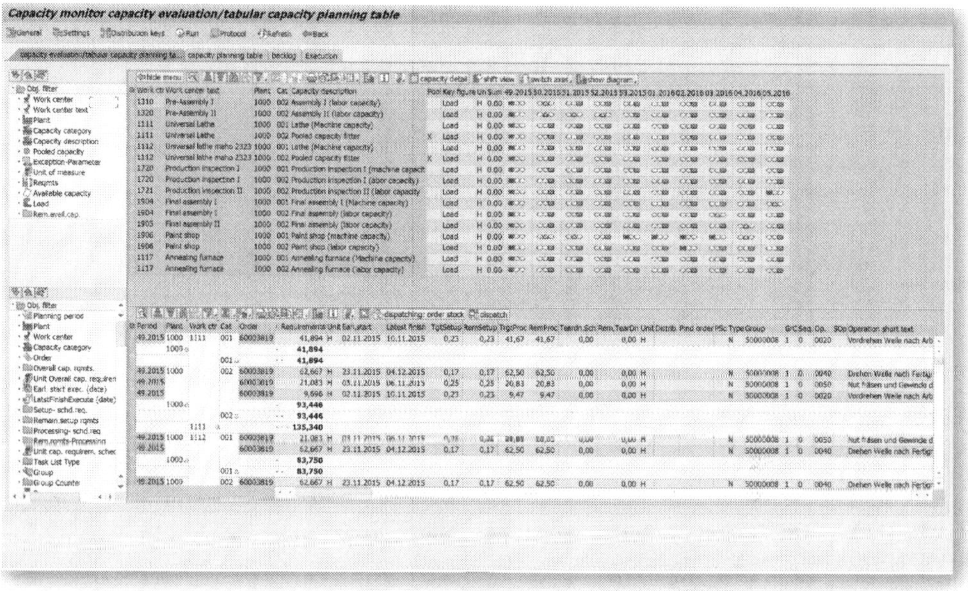

Figure 2.39: SAP Add-On Tool 'Capacity Requirements Monitor'

You might also pick an alternative work center with remaining available capacity, for example, by calling up the planning table using a work center hierarchy

Leveling in transaction CM25 can be done manually or automatically by using the dispatch function. When you level manually you simply drag the order bars from the pool in the lower window and drop them onto the work center in the upper window. Automatic dispatching occurs when you select one or more order bars in the lower window and then push the dispatch button. This distributes (dispatch, level) the orders on the designated work center according to the setting in the strategy profile. In this profile, you have to set the scheduling direction (forward or backward), perform a sort sequence and decide if you want to do finite scheduling—among other things.

A planning log is written for all planning activities so that you can view possible errors during dispatching and take action to resolve them.

2.4   Finite capacity scheduling

Once sequencing and leveling have been done, the orders are distributed within an available capacity profile and can then be scheduled in time. To do this, a start and an end date are determined and saved for each order.

There are a few things to note about scheduling orders in SAP ERP. In the following section, I'll discuss how to rearrange and reschedule orders; how exactly the system uses the individual time elements in routing, work center and order; and the various scheduling types you have at your disposal.

2.4.1   Deallocating and rescheduling

The action of deallocating orders is used when, instead of rearranging or rescheduling the order in time, it is taken out of the finite resource schedule altogether. Often this is done when capacity is too tight to fit an order in with rescheduling.

The easiest way to deallocate an order is by selecting it and hitting the deallocation button. This takes the order from the work center's schedule and puts it back into the order pool in the lower window so that it can be dispatched anew.

Rescheduling an order means rearranging it within the finite resource schedule—filling an open gap or moving it to an earlier or later point in time. Rescheduling can be done either manually—simply drag the order to a new, open point in time—or automatically.

Figure 2.40 schematizes the processes of rescheduling and deallocating because it can be done in the graphical planning tables. As you can see, rescheduling an order means moving its operation(s) backward or forward in time in the finite schedule of a work center. When rescheduling operations, gaps may appear. In the strategy profile of the graphical planning table, you can click on the key 'close gaps' so that the system is able to create a continuous process without gaps.

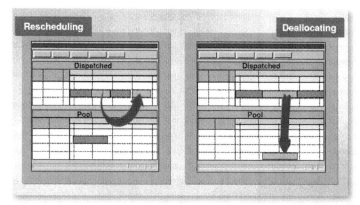

Figure 2.40: Rescheduling and deallocating orders in the graphical planning table

When deallocating operations, the current dispatching dates and 'dis-patched' status are reversed.

2.4.2 Time elements and lead time scheduling

When the system performs lead time scheduling (in a production or planned order), various time elements from the routing, material master or the work center are used to calculate operation and order lead time. Figure 2.41 provides an overview of these time elements.

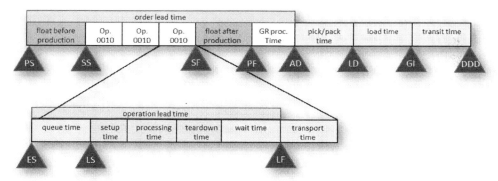

Figure 2.41: Time elements in the order

Each operation has its own time elements. These are the standard values (e.g. setup, processing and teardown) from the routing through to

101

the standard value key and queue time, wait time and transport time coming from the work center. Queue, wait and transport times represent the interoperation times by which the operation's earliest start, latest start and latest finish (ES, LS, LF) are calculated.

In addition to the sequence of operations, you can use order floats (from the scheduling margin key in the material master) which determine the order's planned and scheduled start and end dates (PS, SS, PF, SF). After the GOODS RECEIPT PROCESSING time, the anticipated availability date (AD) is determined. The load date for shipping (LD), goods issue date (GI) and desired delivery date (DDD) from the SD module (sales & distribution) follow.

2.4.3 Scheduling types

Using different scheduling types, you can determine the search direction for remaining available capacity. In Figure 2.42, you see that the system can search forwards or backwards and dispatch operations whenever available capacity is found.

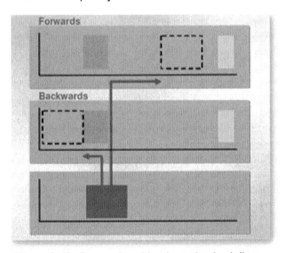

Figure 2.42: Forward and backward scheduling

According to the settings in the dispatching profile, the system can also change planning direction and search in the opposite direction if no available capacity is found by looking in the primary direction.

Another scheduling type is represented by mid-point scheduling. In this method, an operation running on a bottleneck work center (in the middle of a sequence of operations) can be dispatched and capacity leveled first. The system then schedules all previous and subsequent operations from the dispatched operation forwards and backwards in time. In this case, it is assumed that once the bottleneck capacity situation is resolved, all other operations will find enough available capacity and can be scheduled accordingly.

2.5   Capacity evaluation

To evaluate the capacity situation on a shop floor, SAP ERP provides a number of transactions; these can be seen with their transaction codes in Figure 2.43.

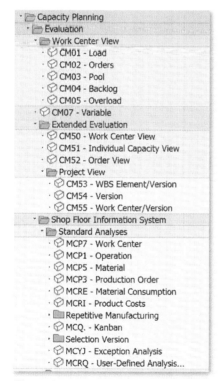

Figure 2.43: Transaction codes to evaluate capacity

For example, you can use transaction CM01 to evaluate the load over a certain period. In Figure 2.44, an overload in machine capacity category 001 is shown (in red) from Week 52, 2015 to Week 07, 2016. The pooled labor capacity 002 shows an overload only in Week 52.

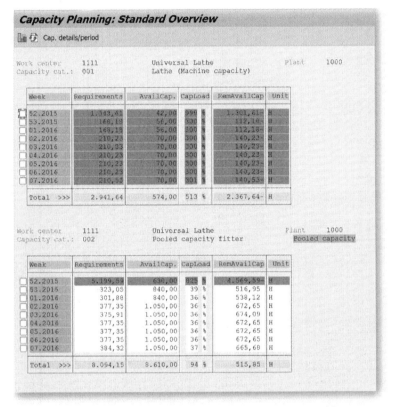

Figure 2.44: Capacity overloads in Week 52 through Week 07

By selecting Week 52 under machine capacity 001 you can further evaluate the overload and display the specific orders which are causing the overload, as shown in Figure 2.45.

An excellent alternative to the somewhat rudimentary capacity evaluation using CM01 is the use of the SAP Add-On Tool[5] 'Capacity Requirements

---

[5] SAP Add-On Tools are additional functions provided by SAP Consulting. SAP Add-On Tools are developed within the SAP namespace but need to be installed separately.

Monitor'. The CRM tool allows for parallel processing of capacity evaluation and capacity leveling. One of its best features is a 'heat map' whereby overloads are indicated with a red light on work centers and periods. A bottleneck can therefore be quickly identified, as shown in Figure 2.46.

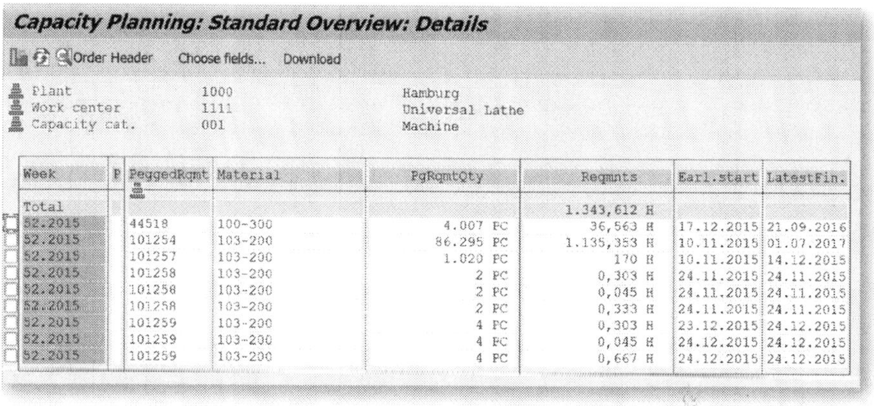

Week	P	PeggedRqmt	Material	PgRqmtQty	Reqmnts	Earl.start	LatestFin.
Total					1.343,612 H		
52.2015		44518	100-300	4.007 PC	36,563 H	17.12.2015	21.09.2016
52.2015		101254	103-200	86.295 PC	1.135,353 H	10.11.2015	01.07.2017
52.2015		101257	103-200	1.020 PC	170 H	10.11.2015	14.12.2015
52.2015		101258	103-200	2 PC	0,303 H	24.11.2015	24.11.2015
52.2015		101258	103-200	2 PC	0,045 H	24.11.2015	24.11.2015
52.2015		101258	103-200	2 PC	0,333 H	24.11.2015	24.11.2015
52.2015		101259	103-200	4 PC	0,303 H	23.12.2015	24.12.2015
52.2015		101259	103-200	4 PC	0,045 H	24.12.2015	24.12.2015
52.2015		101259	103-200	4 PC	0,667 H	24.12.2015	24.12.2015

Figure 2.45: Orders that cause a capacity overload in Week 52

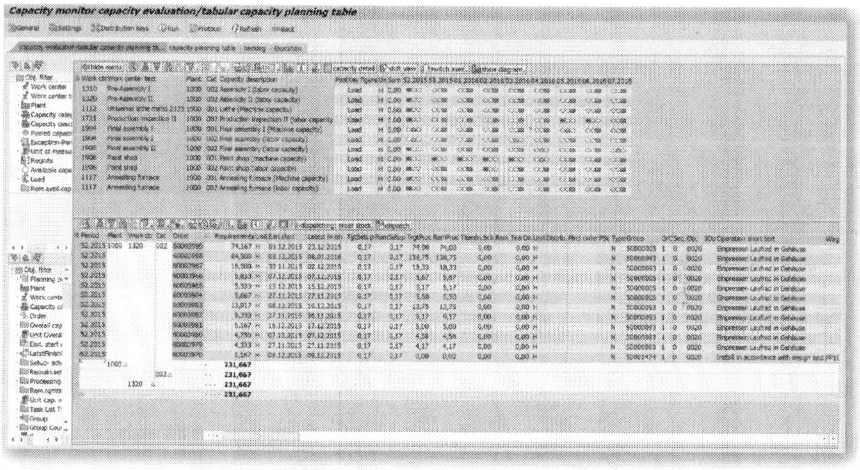

Figure 2.46: SAP Add-On Tool 'Capacity Requirements Monitor'

Subsequently, you can double click on the overloaded work center, list the respective orders and resolve the capacity situation at the same time.

3 Options and Opportunities for Capacity Scheduling in SAP ERP

Let's now take a closer look at the standard functionality of SAP ERP and explore how the theories and processes previously described are configured and executed in the system.

During a typical SAP implementation, the functions and features of capacity scheduling aren't always given top priority. A lack of understanding of the complex and feature-rich functionality to plan, balance, level, sequence and schedule capacity requirements makes it difficult to fully utilize SAP ERP's capacity management module from the very beginning.

Efforts are rarely made to figure out the root causes of ineffective use of capacity. Functions and features are often applied before you even know what's holding up the flow of materials. For example, it's probably not a good idea to decide on a sequencing method such as 'setup optimization' when the true problem lies in the fact that large batches are hindering the flow of materials.

As we know, the SAP ERP system is a tool with which you can create a good process design. For this very reason, process design must come first; a good process design needs experience and intuition so an analyst can build effective solutions which meet today's requirements for demand-driven flow of information and materials.

We live in a complex world and today's supply chains are faced with more complexity than ever. Variability in supply and demand is high and, to make matters worse, managers sometimes create self-inflicted variability by making bad decisions to solve problems. This often happens because we don't necessarily look at the big picture, but rather work in silos. If the problem is late deliveries, the sales department blames production scheduling and asks why the orders weren't finished on time and in full. The order was placed a long time ago and given the appropriate priority, right? From a sales perspective, the shop floor should run according to a sequence of prioritized orders, but in reality, the costing

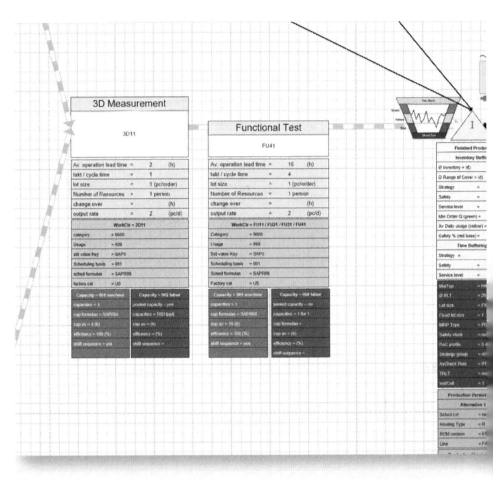

department often dictates that a shop floor utilize resources and capacity to their maximum extent... which might then conflict significantly with a customer's request.

It is therefore important to take a closer look at the bigger picture and pick the appropriate scheduling strategy for the right situation. It is important to note that many different scheduling strategies can be used even within the same factory. For example, the machining part of a production program might be run with a discrete schedule of production orders, the heat treatment with recipes, formulas and process orders, and the final assembly of the product with a takt-based schedule that allows for flow.

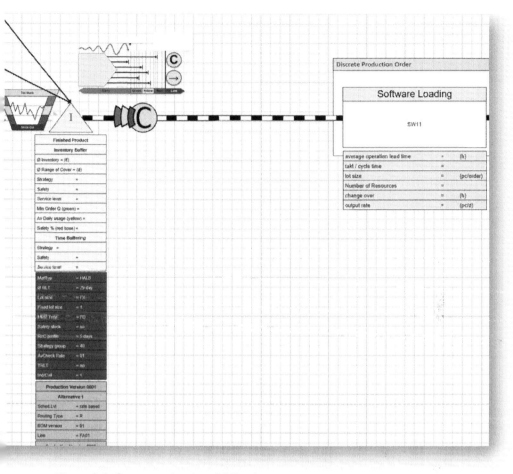

Figure 3.1: Components of an SAP value stream map

In the following section, I'll explore the different features and options you have in standard SAP ERP and what you must set up to achieve maximum automation and usability.

3.1 Finite scheduling of a discrete work center

Discrete production orders are the most commonly used order types in companies using SAP software to run their operations. This does not necessarily mean that it is the appropriate order type for the sort of manufacturing these companies do. However, for the purpose of explaining how to schedule production orders into a finite, capacity-checked schedule, I'm putting aside the discussion about when to use discrete production orders and when not to.

If you're set up for discrete manufacturing, you have created at least one work center but, much more likely, you use quite a large number of work center records to create a sequence of operations for the manufacture of sellable products. Each work center record contains information for capacities, such as labor or machine. The system knows from this when these capacities are available and each order can reserve time on these capacities (at the work center) to execute one or more operations.

Each of these work centers has a fixed location on the shop floor and the routing of each product connects these work centers into a flow through their operations (which run on a specific work center). A value stream map is an excellent way to visualize such flows.

Figure 3.1 shows an example of a value stream map with specific work centers and a master data setup with buffering.

You can now build the routing based on a defined value stream and Figure 3.2 shows an example of this with operations and assigned work centers.

Change Rate Routing: Operation Overview

Material 13	Generic OW SL	Grp.Count1
Sequence 0	FINAL ASSEMBLY	

Operation Overv.

Act	SOp	Ref. Ta...	R...	Work ctr	Takt	Ltkt	N.	Co...	C.	O.	L.	P.	Operation short text	C.	B...	Un	N...	R...	Production ...	U...	Seti
0010				ASSY01		0		FPG1					Avio & Payload coupling		1	EA			200	MIN	
0020				ASSY01	1	1		FPG1					Avio & payload coupling 2		1	EA			40	MIN	
0030				ASSY02		0		FPG1					Propulsion coupling		1	EA			300	MIN	
0040				ASSY03		0		FPG1					Batteries & MLI		1	EA			120	MIN	
0050				ASSY03		0		FPG1					Batteries & MLI 2		1	EA			120	MIN	
0060				ASSY04		0		FPG1					SAWM coupling		1	EA			300	MIN	
0070				ASSY05		0		FPG1					Test		1	EA			100	MIN	
0080				ASSY05		0		FPG1					Test		1	EA			200	MIN	
0090						0									1	EA					

Figure 3.2: Routing in SAP

As mentioned before, the work center holds the available working time or, in other words, available capacity. This means that the system knows the available capacity of a certain work center for a certain period. In order to figure out if an order fits into the available production time before its desired finish, you must calculate a utilization for that period and ensure that the utilization doesn't exceed 100%.

Side note: utilization

 Most cost accounting strategies ask for high utilization on production lines. More often than not, this conflicts with the desire and need for demand-driven flow on the shop floor. When lines are utilized to their maximum, a little variation in demand, supply or on the work center can cause havoc to the production line. Even worse, the higher the utilization, the higher the impact of variability. As utilization approaches 100%, the delay caused by variability is infinite. Every good plan includes a buffer in the planned utilization and never schedules to 100% or higher.

When the utilization is set, you can enter it in the work center and make working time available for the period that you're planning for.

The detailed, time-based capacity planning approach we're referring to here is usually applied to a short-term planning horizon. Within this horizon, you take the planned orders that the MRP Run generated and space them out so that they fit within the available hours on the work center. In discrete capacity planning, you take a pool of lead time scheduled planned orders and schedule a work center which those orders all have in common. This is usually the bottleneck work center.

The bottleneck work center is the work center that exhibits the biggest load or highest utilization in a group of products for a specific period of time (in this case, the short-term planning horizon).

To execute this activity (leveling of discrete planned orders) in SAP you use transaction CM25, which provides you with a graphical planning board.

What we can see in Figure 3.3 is a leveled order sequence for two weeks. The top window shows the start and end dates and times for the sequenced operation, whereas the bottom window displays the products and how they were put in order.

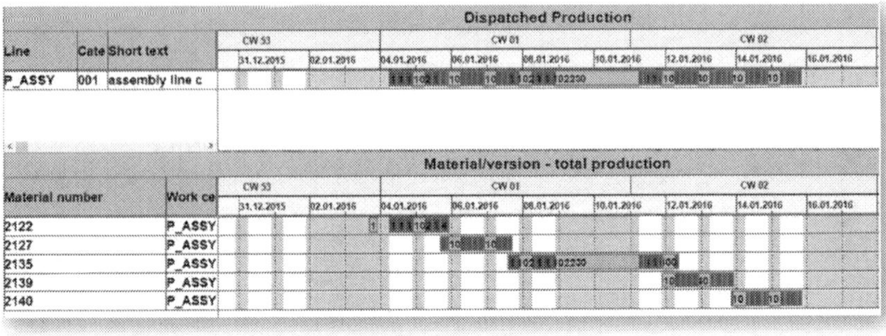

Figure 3.3: Capacity leveling with transaction CM25

Note that only one operation from each planned order was leveled. During saving, the system sets start and end dates for the orders by rescheduling them mid-point.

Finite scheduling of a discrete work center simply means that we take the infinite plan that the MRP Run generated (planned orders that are stacked up on top of each other according to their latest end date and are scheduled backwards) and space them out to fit into the available working hours on the bottleneck work center.

The orders are now fixed and finite, so next they'll ask for materials to be issued to specific operations. Because we did finite scheduling, the requirements dates for the parts and materials are now set to the correct date (they weren't correct before finite scheduling) and therefore you're able to carry out a collective material availability check for all the fixed (and capacity checked) planned orders in the production schedule.

The code for the collective availability check is transaction MDVP. It provides you with a missing parts list so that you can expedite materials that are not yet available. As a suggestion, you should consider not releasing any production orders to the floor which do not have all the required materials available. Releasing an order with missing parts would mean that the order gets stuck and blocks any other orders that could flow through.

After checking collective materials availability and expediting missing parts you can now collectively convert the planned orders into production orders and also release them. The respective codes are transaction CO41 for the collective conversion, and transaction CO05N to collectively release production orders.

3.2 Takt-based sequencing and scheduling of a flow line

Most assembly lines flow best when they're scheduled by a pre-determined takt. Intuitively, most production schedulers seek to drive the flow using a takt, but they only very rarely use standard SAP functionality to do so. For some reason, takt-based scheduling of flow lines is one of the best kept secrets in SAP functionality. It is poorly documented and not many consultants or users know how to set it up.

Before I go into the details around configuring and using a takt-based schedule, let's revisit some basic concepts and theories around flowing assembly lines.

An assembly line is an object which supports a manufacturing process in which parts are added as the semi-finished (sub) assembly moves from workstation to workstation. During the flow, parts are added in sequence until the final assembly is complete. Therefore, a finished product can be assembled faster and with less labor than by having workers carry parts to a stationary work center. Henry Ford perfected the assembly line by installing driven conveyor belts that could produce a Model T in 93 minutes. The assembly line developed for the Ford Model T began operation on December 1, 1913.

Examples of these assembly lines can be found in the automotive industry where certain steps in the assembly line are scheduled to install the engine, install the hood, and install the wheels—in that order. Only one of these steps can be done at a time. In traditional production, only one car would be assembled at a time. If engine installation takes 20 minutes, hood installation takes 5 minutes, and wheel installation takes 10 minutes, then a car can be produced every 35 minutes. In a takt-based assembly line, car assembly is split between several stations, all working simultaneously. When one station is finished with a car, it passes it on to the next. With three stations, a total of three different cars can be assembled on the line at the same time, each one at a different assembly stage. 'Takt' introduces protection to the work content at each station of the assembly line (e.g. 20 minutes, 5 minutes, 10 minutes) so that parts can flow. In our example, the takt of the line must be equal to, or greater than, 20 minutes so that all three operations can flow along the line without interruption.

Takt is usually calculated according to customer demand at a given period of time. Because it represents the inverse of the throughput rate, the minimum takt time is bound by the maximum output rate of the line. For example, a car due for assembly is introduced as a job onto the line every 30 minutes. If everything flows, the line will put out 2 cars per hour. However, the line itself has limited production; i.e. a maximum rate, which is bound by how much work content can be attained on each station. If the line can produce 4 cars per hour you can run the line with a takt of 15 minutes, but if the line can only handle 1 car per hour you cannot run the line faster than with a takt of 60 minutes; i.e. introduce a new car assembly job onto the first work station every hour.

However, automobile assembly lines are definitely not the only assembly lines which profit from takt-based scheduling. This type of schedule can be used wherever flow is the paramount objective. Think of packaging lines for food manufacturers, power transformers, big circuit breakers or even an aircraft's FAL (final assembly line) with tens of thousands of operations. The latter is hard to imagine but so much more efficient with a line routing and REM (repetitive manufacturing) orders than by means of thousands of discrete production orders which must be balanced and sequenced using functionality outside of SAP (probably Excel spreadsheets).

I have spoken to many organizations about this type of scheduling and, particularly when a product is highly customizable, managers tend to doubt that this is the best way to go. I always argue that a generic takt is much more flexible and easier to plan than a discrete length of an operation. To that extent, I'd like to outline the difference between lead time scheduling and takt-based scheduling.

The difference between lead time scheduling and takt-based scheduling

 Lead time scheduling is done when you create a production order in SAP. You can also run lead time scheduling during the generation of a planned order when you set the Scheduling Indicator in the MRP Run to '2'. Lead time scheduling simply takes the required delivery date of to the demand and performs backward scheduling via the valid routing operations. After lead time scheduling, the order has scheduled start and end dates in addition to the basic start and end dates. Lead time scheduling is illustrated in Figure 3.4:

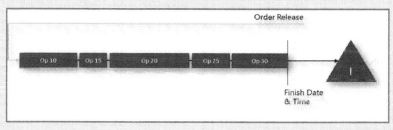

Figure 3.4: Lead time scheduling

Takt-based scheduling, on the other hand, looks at how much time is *required* within a period and how much time is *available* in the same period. Once we know this, we can calculate how long an item in production can spend on each station so that it still flows fast enough to meet the demand on time. In takt-based scheduling, we have to ensure that the operations fit into the takt or work content. The activity of distributing the operations into the available work content is called Line Balancing and is, in fact, the flow line's capacity planning.

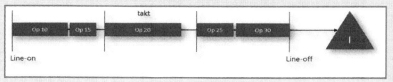

Figure 3.5: Takt-based scheduling

When you are dealing with highly customized products and you need to plan ahead, it is much easier to plan generic work content with an estimated takt (meeting estimated customer demand) than to schedule the specific lead times of all the different operations every time a change occurs. In other words, a takt-based schedule, as shown in Figure 3.5, serves as a placeholder for capacity where the actual configuration can be dropped in at a later point in time when the specific configuration is known.

Now that we have defined the difference between takt and lead time scheduling, let's have a closer look at takt-based scheduling:

Takt-based scheduling requires SAP's tools of repetitive manufacturing because otherwise you can't create a sequence schedule. The first thing that needs to be set up is a line hierarchy. Line hierarchies are created using transaction LDB1 and represent the assembly line with all its work centers. Note that the line hierarchy does **not** represent the flow of the product but rather represents the hierarchy of the work centers the product flows through (or doesn't flow through). The line hierarchy can consist of line segments and feeder work centers assigned to a level-by-level hierarchical structure. An example is shown in Figure 3.6.

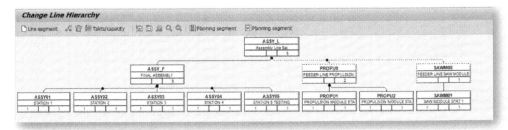

Figure 3.6: Line hierarchy created with transaction LDB1

The line hierarchy can have a scheduling segment (usually the bottleneck work center) that is then used in the production version of the materials being assembled on the line. In the production version, you also assign the routing that is used to assemble the product. You can use a regular routing (type N) but for repetitive manufacturing a rate routing (type R) is recommended. As a native German speaker, I much prefer the German term 'Linienplan' and believe that the English translation 'line routing' (as opposed to 'rate routing') much better describes what this is: a sequence of operations that follows the assembly line.

Figure 3.7 is an example of a line routing with two feeder lines in a graphical display.

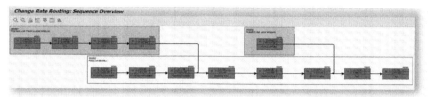

Figure 3.7: A line routing with feeder lines

Figure 3.8 shows how the production version should be maintained.

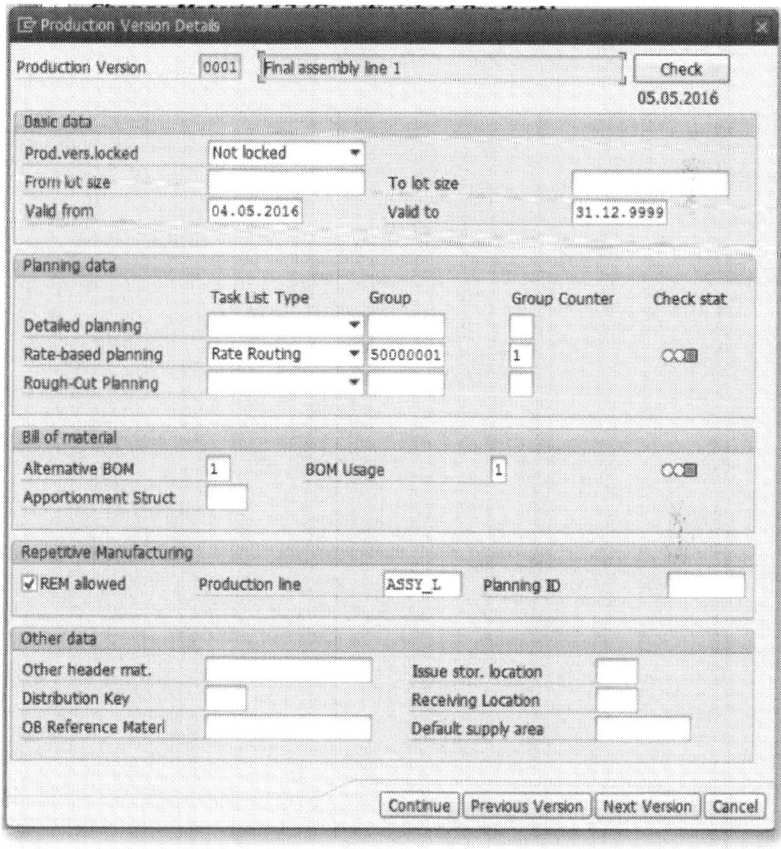

Figure 3.8: Production version with a line routing and a production line for takt-based scheduling

Once a line routing (using the work centers of a line hierarchy) exists, we can perform line balancing. Transaction LDD1 is used in line balancing to calculate a takt based on the demand for the product mix within a certain period. In the following example, a takt time of 6 hours and 28 minutes has been calculated. This means that the orders for the products in the mix enter the line once every 6 hours and 28 minutes (see Figure 3.9).

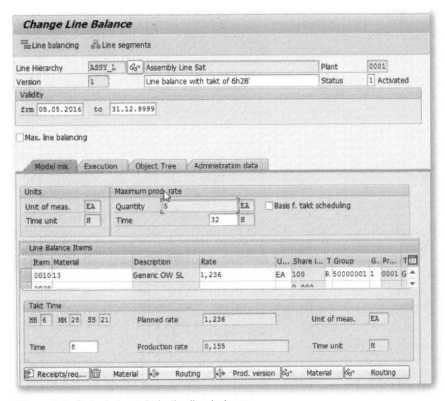

Figure 3.9: Calculating takt in the line balance

Line balancing also allows operations to be distributed within the takt time onto the various stations so that no takt violations occur. The distribution can be done in a graphical interface, as shown in Figure 3.10.

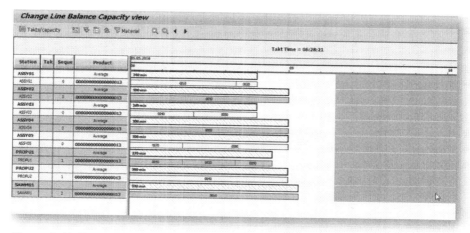

Figure 3.10: Takt-based line balancing

In Figure 3.10, there is no takt violation as all operations fit into the takt of their assigned stations. If there were a takt violation (i.e. an operation extending into the grey area to the right) you could pick up that operation and move it onto a station where there is space to execute it. Dragging and dropping an operation to another station also updates the line routing.

Note that there can be many routings from a product mix balanced in this graphic.

After the assembly line is balanced for the next period according to the predetermined takt, we can then schedule from week to week. This simply means that we spread the orders in a sequencing schedule according to the takt, or timespan, from order to order. This can be done using transactions MF50 or LAS2.

The scheduling result can be seen in Figure 3.11.

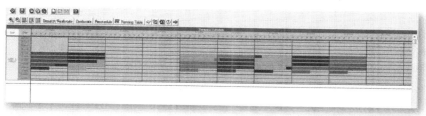

Figure 3.11: Takt-based sequencing schedule

119

This example shows a line-on view of the assembly line and the intervals at which the individual orders enter the first station of the line. It shows the exact time the orders come onto the first work center.

Note that the length of the bar does **not** represent the lead time of the order, but rather the length of time the order spends on the first station before it moves onto the second station, or work center, in the line hierarchy. Therefore, you are looking at a release schedule that is driven by the takt time.

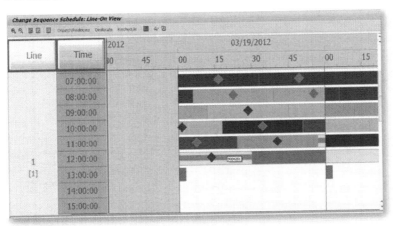

Figure 3.12: Details of a sequence schedule

Figure 3.12 depicts the possible information you could put on a sequence schedule. In this case, a different color is assigned to each material on the schedule. A diamond symbol is used to indicate results from the material availability check. A red diamond means the availability check failed and there are missing parts. A green diamond means that the availability check returned a positive result, and all parts are available for the order.

Another symbol is the thin, red bar laid over the thick, yellow bar. It indicates whether we are adhering to a customer order's requested delivery date, or not. Red means we're behind schedule, green means we're ahead of schedule and yellow would depict that we're right on time.

To summarize takt-based scheduling of a flow line, you start by calculating a takt time based on the demand for the period of evaluation. Then you ensure that all operations fit into that takt time. This process is called line balancing. Once the line is balanced with the orders that need to run for that period, you pick the frozen zone period and schedule and space the orders (generated by the MRP Run) according to the takt time.

The resulting production schedule is then printed and handed to the shop floor for execution.

Contrary to popular belief, this type of scheduling can be used for a wide variety of products. We have applied takt-based schedules to numerous products from high-volume, very repetitive shower heads or brake pads to highly customizable specialty vehicles (e.g. ambulances, RV's, fire trucks), power transformers and even satellites.

Takt-based scheduling provides tremendous opportunities for all types of manufacturers and is vastly underutilized in SAP. That's why I have dedicated a large part of this book to this topic.

3.3 Takt-based scheduling of a flow line with Kanban withdrawals

Another variation of takt-based scheduling is the scheduling of a flow line, whereby the signal to produce does not come from a forecast but from a Kanban control cycle and a container being set to 'empty'.

Kanban, as discussed later in this chapter, is a visual control mechanism where the signal to replenish does not come from a system signal but from a void on the demand side of a replenishment cycle. In the cycle, you define how much product must be available on one side (the demand side) and when and how much is to be replenished from the other side (the supply side).

A downside of the Kanban process for triggering production is that the replenishment orders triggered by Kanban have no sequence by which they're supposed to be executed. When the replenishment signal is triggered, an order is generated and forward scheduled from today's date. Available capacity and the sequence that orders should go into production are not considered. It's simply a list of orders that need to be replenished NOW!

I'd now like to introduce a concept where we combine the advantages of a visual, real-time replenishment process with the need for sequencing and scheduling.

We start with a forecast and run MRP to create planned orders within the short-term planning horizon. Subsequently, a takt is calculated in line balancing and the operations are graphically displayed to avoid any takt violations occurring. After the line is balanced for the period in question, we start the planning process by sequencing and scheduling the planned orders with the takt. As a result, we have a production plan: a sequence schedule that could look something like the image in Figure 3.13.

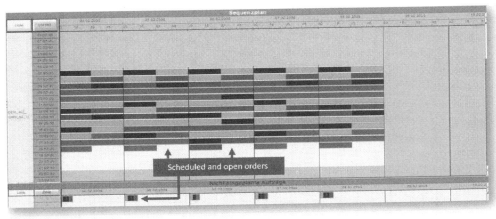

Figure 3.13: Planned sequencing schedule

In Figure 3.13, a line-on view shows a sequence of planned orders spread out according to the previously calculated takt. Note that these orders do not fulfill actual requirements, but rather cover a forecasted demand that might or might not be fulfilled as planned.

According to our concept, these orders and the entire schedule are simply created as placeholders waiting for actual demand to occur. Because we've combined this plan with a Kanban control cycle for the products to be manufactured, any void on the demand side of the cycle now attaches itself to this plan.

In a regular control cycle, a void would result in the generation of a new replenishment order. However, in our control cycle this is not the case. Where any void is reported, you look at the schedule to find an order that covers the requirement for that specific product and attach it to that order instead of creating a new one.

We can visualize this type of order in the sequence schedule. This is done by overlaying a thin, blue bar on the product bar, as shown in Figure 3.14.

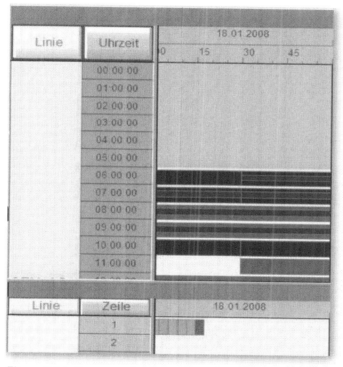

Figure 3.14: Sequenced order assigned to a Kanban control cycle

We now have an order that is scheduled, sequenced and assigned to fill a Kanban void on the demand side. This concept enables you to produce a plan, reserve capacity on the line, procure all the necessary materials and, most importantly, only trigger production when there is actual demand.

This adheres to the principles of demand-driven manufacturing.

3.4 Scheduling a mixed model production line with MTS and MTO

Another option to run a takt-based line is using a mix of models. Mixed model production means running a schedule that includes different variations of a product or different products altogether. Imagine shower heads—there might be a number of different models but they all follow roughly the same sequence of operations. Or, consider sub-assemblies in aircraft manufacturing—you might want to assemble pylons for the A318, A319 and A320 on the same assembly line. So, if you have different demands for different pylons, you must figure out how much of each type you have to put together in any given planning and execution week.

Heijunka—the scheduling of rates according to equal distribution—is such a mixed model scheduling method. This method follows the principle of EPEI (Every Part Every Interval). If your intervals are days and you schedule for a week, then you'd assemble at least one pylon for each type of aircraft every day. In fact, you'd look at the demand of the total week and then distribute the rates according to EPEI. Let's look at an example.

Figure 3.15 shows weekly demand for three different pylons.

Figure 3.15: Weekly demand for three different types

First, we must split the demand into lot sizes that allow equal distribution, as shown in Figure 3.16. The MRP Run does that for us; it takes the total weekly demand and splits it into individual planned orders according to the Lot Sizing procedure we maintained in the MRP1 screen of the material master record.

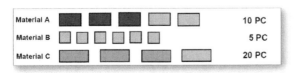

Figure 3.16: Split lot sizes after the MRP Run

We can then distribute these individual lots equally across each day's schedule. This can be done automatically if we employ a heijunka strategy in transaction LAS2 or in MF50 with sequencing (see Figure 3.17).

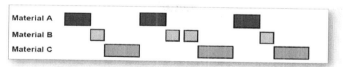

Figure 3.17: Equal distribution (EPEI) according to a heijunka strategy

To show how this looks in practice in SAP, we can create a model mix using transaction LDD1 (to create) or LDD2 (to maintain), as shown in Figure 3.18. A prerequisite for line balancing is the existence of a line hierarchy with a maximum rate.

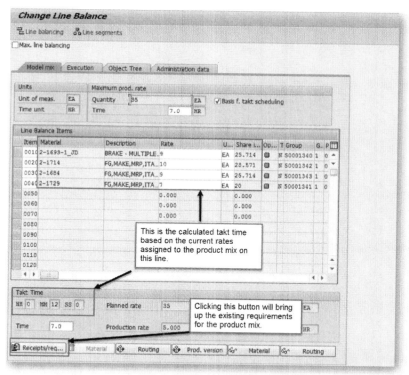

Figure 3.18: The model mix and a calculated takt time

If the planned rate exceeds the maximum rate, you can make some adjustments in the individual material's rates until they match up.

Once the rate is set and the takt is calculated (to meet the demanded output rates, as per our example), we must run the line at a takt of 12 minutes; i.e. every 12 minutes a job is introduced to the line and we must balance the line. This can be done using a graphical interface that can be accessed by clicking on 'Line balancing', as shown in Figure 3.19.

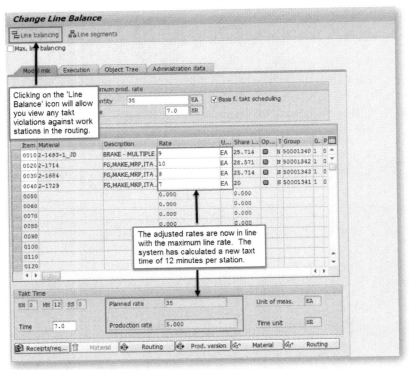

Figure 3.19: Setting takt and rates

In the graphical view of the line balance, as in Figure 3.20, we can see all stations (work centers) and if we expand the view of the station, we can see the operations for each product when they are running on the line.

This view allows you to see the length of the takt. Because station 65030TRY has three takts, its takt time is 36 minutes and more work content fits on it. Because the individual products running through that station are broken down in the view, you can see that the four products—154, 181, 184 and 188—are all loading the station with different operations. For the first product, 154, its operation 0070 takes up 24 minutes and fits well into the takt time. Both products 181 and 184 also have an operation 0070 running on station 65030TRY, but the work content of these operations is so low that it takes up only 2 and 3 minutes respectively of the available takt time of 36 minutes.

To make matters worse, operation 0080 for product 188, is too long and therefore violates the takt time.

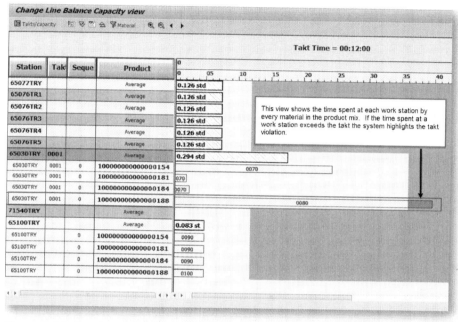

Figure 3.20: Graphical view of line balancing

We can see in the example in Figure 3.20 that the line is not balanced well enough to run the model mix efficiently. You have to break up operations, move them to another station where they fit, or fill up the takt time for the other products in the mix.

All of this can be done using 'drag and drop' in the line balancing transaction LDD1 and therefore represents the takt-based scheduling's capacity planning as shown in Figure 3.20. If you change the sequence of the operations or assign the operation to another work center, you will actually update the materials routing.

Once line balancing is done and the takt is calculated, you release (acti-vate) the line balance as a usable version and move on to scheduling the model mix.

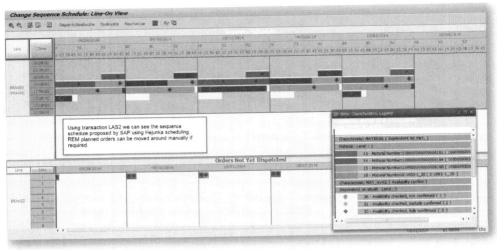

Figure 3.21: Mixed model, takt-based sequencing schedule

In Figure 3.21, you can see the result of scheduling from transaction LAS2. Here, we have used the takt from the released line balancing rec-ord that is valid for a specific period and sequenced all the planned or-ders for all the materials in the model mix.

Note that the orders were spaced according to the takt time and you can now see when each order is supposed to come onto the first station on the production line. Each material in the model mix is assigned its own color and a diamond has been placed on the bars so we can see wheth-er parts are available or not.

Mixed model scheduling is an easy and effective way to create flow into your supply chain while meeting demand on time.

3.5   Product wheel scheduling for the process industry

Product wheel scheduling is a concept which allows for standardized, noise-reduced production of fast and slow moving products made to stock and made to order. It first came about as a tool to introduce the 'lean' principle to process manufacturers, primarily in the automotive industry. Product wheels have now found widespread acceptance in the chemical, pharmaceutical and food processing industries as they allow for the scheduling of large batches and take into consideration the difficulties of switching over from one product batch to another.

There are some specifics to be considered when using the product wheel in process industries and I'd like to provide you with some ideas on how a product wheel could be configured into SAP. Figure 3.22 shows an example of a product wheel.

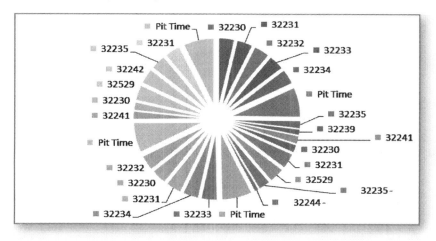

Figure 3.22: A product wheel

3.5.1 What is product wheel scheduling?

If your company is a process manufacturer, you most likely mix, blend, cure or otherwise process your products on a production line. One of the characteristics of processed products is that you can't disassemble them (orange juice can't be made back into oranges, for example). Compare this with bicycle production—you can usually 'unscrew' a bicycle and put the components back into inventory (even though this is not 100% true, it is an approximate way of differentiating between process and discrete manufacturing).

There is a scheduling concept that finds widespread adoption in discrete industries: it is called The Rhythm Wheel and it provides a number of advantages. For the process industry, we can use the same kind of concept. However, because of the specifics of the process industry (longer run times for batches, more complex change overs, etc.) a slightly different process is required. That process is defined by the concept of Product Wheel scheduling.

With this concept, the circle represents the lengths of the planning cycle (see Figure 3.23). A complete description of this concept can be found in Section 2.2.3 'The product wheel'.

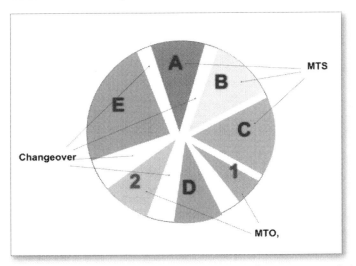

Figure 3.23: Product wheel with MTO and MTS segments and changeover spaces

The product wheel is a production scheduling method based on average demand, but which is executed for actual demand. The phases for a product wheel are:

1. Identify the location (line or line segment) on your production floor where the product wheel is to be used for scheduling.

2. Design a standard sequence using all the products which can be produced on the line.

3. Determine the lengths and frequencies of the wheel's cycle.

4. Schedule or load the product wheel for the next cycle so that it meets planned demand.

5. Execute the schedule for the cycle according to the plan and fulfill incoming orders from inventory.

The last point is particularly important because it follows the core philosophy of product wheel scheduling:

Produce the product to inventory according to a predefined plan in the frozen zone, and fulfill actual demand from inventory which was replenished from the previous production cycle.

Product wheel scheduling brings transparency and insights that help to continuously optimize the way we produce. A uniform, level production schedule maximizes equipment and labor utilization, and smooths out requirements for raw materials. One of lean manufacturing's major changes in thinking involves taking variable demand and finding a way to distribute it evenly. Product wheel scheduling does exactly that. It moves away from scheduling customer demand on an instantaneous basis, and integrates the variable demand into a longer time frame.

3.5.2 Implementing the product wheel with SAP

First, we must perform a segmentation to classify our manufactured products into four categories:

▶ MTS high volume, every cycle—these are your front running items. You maintain an inventory level which provides high availability (high service levels) to your customers.

▶ MTS low volume, every other cycle—these products are demanded less frequently and find their way onto the product wheel only every other cycle, or possibly only every third or fourth cycle.

▶ Breach of inventory requirement—these products are only demanded from time to time. However, we cannot afford to delay production until we have the customer order in place because our customers would not accept having to wait out the replenishment time, and instead would buy from another producer. Therefore, we keep some inventory for these products and trigger more production based on a breach of a reorder point.

131

▶ MTO—products with infrequent demand which happen to be valuable, perishable and/or relatively quick to replenish—we trigger production only when a customer order is present.

While performing the segmentation, you need to consider some determining factors that can be described as follows:

▶ cost of inventory—requires short cycles

▶ cost of changeover—requires long cycles

▶ shelf life—requires short cycles

▶ short-term product demand variability

▶ minimum practical lot size

Then you must define some standards before you can use the product wheel for production scheduling. An annual strategy meeting is the best time to set the wheel's cycle duration and performance boundaries and identify the places where the wheel will be used for scheduling.

Once these decisions are made, you can implement the standard steps and sequence with which a planner can design and subsequently run or schedule the product wheel. Some of the steps to implement product wheel scheduling are given below:

1. Create an SAP Value Stream Map with all master data, decoupling points and pacemaker / wheel locations.

2. Where on the floor? Decide on the locations where you want to run product wheel scheduling.

3. Set up demand volume and segmentation—perform the segmentation as described above.

4. Decide sequencing—establish a changeover matrix.

5. Determine wheel time (cycle)—consider: fastest, most economical, shelf life, demand variability, minimum lot size.

6. Establish wheel frequency for each product.

7. Distribute products across cycles—balance cycle to cycle.

8. Visualize wheel cycles—diagrams.

9. Calculate inventory requirements.

To define the standard sequence, proceed as follows:

A standard sequence provides a template for the actual sequence. In it we identify all products which could ever run on the line and provide a mechanism which every actual sequence will follow, with only those products on the schedule which are actually demanded in that cycle.

To set a standard sequence in SAP, we use the setup matrix fields SET-UP GROUP CATEGORY and SETUP GROUP KEY. Configuring the field's settings in SAP's customization enables us to define each product's place in the sequence. This is done in the product's standard routing or recipe. Go to the sequence of operations and from there drill down into the details of the operation with your production line. In there, you find the fields SETUP GROUP CATEGORY and SETUP GROUP KEY. From the list of options, pick those values which place the product you are maintaining into the right place in the sequence, as shown in Figure 3.24: Setup group category value.

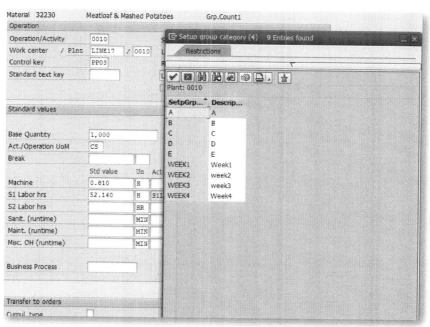

Figure 3.24: Setup group category value.

For the routing displayed here we pick Group 'C' in setup group category, which places the product at the top of the sequence. Next, we pick the setup group key.

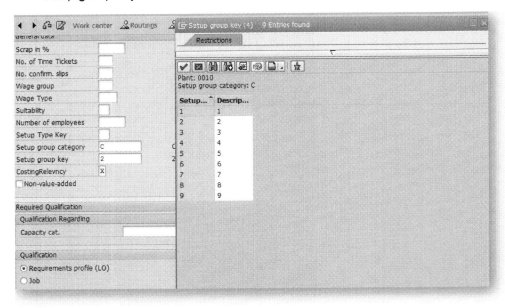

Figure 3.25: Setup group key values

Value 2 is picked here (see Figure 3.25), which places the product in second place within the third group 'C' of the sequence.

If you continue assigning setup group category (the group) and setup group key (the sequence within the group) to the routings of the materials you manufacture, you build a standard sequence by which these products fall into place should they be demanded and a planned order occurs.

Next, I'll demonstrate how orders can be scheduled using this sequence by way of the DISPATCH SEQUENCE in SAP's scheduling transaction CM25.

3.5.3 Product wheel scheduling with CM25

After all settings (changeover matrix, sequence schedule, routing data, material master record) have been set up, we can then schedule the infinite supply plan, generated by the MRP Run, into a finite supply plan using transaction CM25.

You can see in Figure 3.26 that all generated, unscheduled planned orders are visible in the order pool in the bottom window.

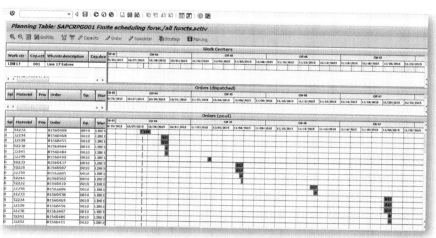

Figure 3.26: Planned orders, unscheduled, in the order pool

We need to pick the frozen zone period and schedule relevant orders (i.e. within the time period) from the pool onto the processing line. This must be done within available capacity and in the correct sequence.

To determine the correct sequence, we must choose the dispatch key that uses the changeover matrix we configured in the system. This is done using the strategy profile, as shown in Figure 3.27.

135

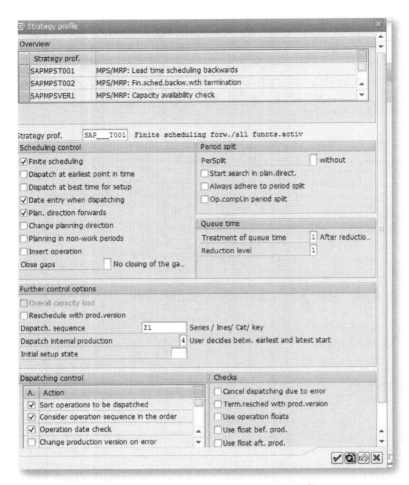

Figure 3.27: Dispatch sequence Z2 in the strategy profile

You can now select all the relevant planned orders from the pool and push the dispatch button. This distributes the orders in a given sequence, within the available capacity, on the processing line.

The result can be seen in Figure 3.28.

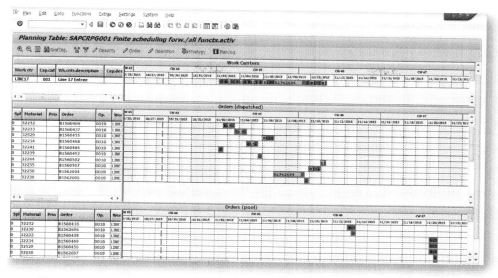

Figure 3.28: Dispatched, finite product wheel schedule

Product wheel scheduling can be highly automated in SAP if you set up all the relevant master data upfront.

In the next chapter, I'll outline how you can create a product wheel schedule for discrete industries.

3.6 Product wheel scheduling for discrete parts production

Product wheel scheduling can be set up for discrete manufacturing in a very similar way to that described above for process manufacturing. However, since discrete manufacturing doesn't require the use of batch sizes (which has a derogatory effect in many cases) it makes sense to look at a slightly different setup.

There's a lot of talk about pull systems as the current solution for all problems. I'd like to point out a few things about the product wheel (rhythm wheel) approach because it relates to being demand-driven (or 'pull'). A pull-based production control system is not induced by SOP or MRP, but rather by real consumption or orders triggered by customers. By aligning production output to physical consumption or customer orders, stock levels can be minimized and working capital reduced to its anticipated level.

Because not every material and process can be controlled by a pull-driven concept, hybrid approaches or combinations of push and pull may be more efficient in the overall process. A possible combination of the two different thought systems is done through de-coupling points. A de-coupling point is defined by an inventory buffer. It allows demand and supply variability to be smoothed and leveled. When setting up the necessary buffer, it needs to be dimensioned very carefully because it can be either too small to cope with fluctuation (stockouts occur) or too high (excess stock, increase in working capital and 'waste').

Such a system can be set up and executed using a product or rhythm wheel, which allows for the scheduling and capacity planning of the work going through the de-coupling point.

At this point, I would like to mention SAP Add-On Tools— SAP's instruments which continue to enhance their ECC (Enterprise Central Component) offering. The SAP Add-On Tools enjoy widespread use in Europe and North America, with flagship products such as MRP Monitor, Inventory Controlling Cockpit, Safety Stock Simulation and Forecast Monitor. Not so long ago another great addition was launched—the Lean Manufacturing Planning & Control Tool (LMPC).

The LMPC tool enhances possibilities in SAP ERP standard functionality, and consists of tools from lean manufacturing and classic production planning & control. For example, it offers an additional transaction to level order quantities, as well as an enhanced planning table which can also be used in the traditional way when lean manufacturing methodologies don't apply to the production process.

In this chapter, I suggest using LMPC for product wheel scheduling of discrete products. LMPC allows rhythm wheels to be set up. Figure 3.29 shows that the cycle time (processing time) and setup time of a given period can be spread out over the wheel. In our example, we use four different materials—A, B, C and D, that are demanded over the period in question.

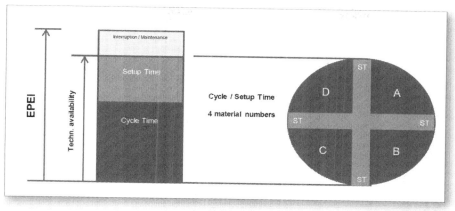

Figure 3.29: Rhythm wheel with four different materials

The basic idea behind the rhythm wheel is to create smaller lot sizes for more flexibility and lower average inventory holdings. Large batches result in longer 'days of inventory holding' and block capacity that might otherwise be used if available.

Distributing smaller quantities reduces inventory holdings more frequently, but the trade-off is that you 'waste' more time with setups. This is shown in Figure 3.30. However, the additional setup time is not necessarily lost time, because using additional capacity to manufacture more product results in overproduction waste.

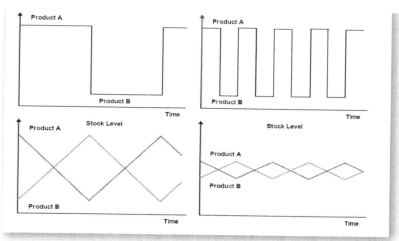

Figure 3.30: Smaller lot sizes more frequently

139

Let's now look at the tool and some of its features.

LMPC comprises an enhanced planning table which is designed as a classic add-on with no required interfaces. It is based on, but not limited to, the features of the standard planning table such as dispatching, de-allocating and rescheduling orders.

In addition to the enhanced functions, it can also be used as a flexible development kit for further customer-specific enhancements. It offers the possibility to create your own screen views and your own actions, and to use additional settings in customizing. It is set up in the default or stand-ard delivery to include a table (ALV-Grid) to show operations (pop-up window), a screen to show user-defined HTML contents and a window to show capacity utilization and stock levels over time.

Figure 3.31 displays the selection screen for the LMPC's EPEI calculation.

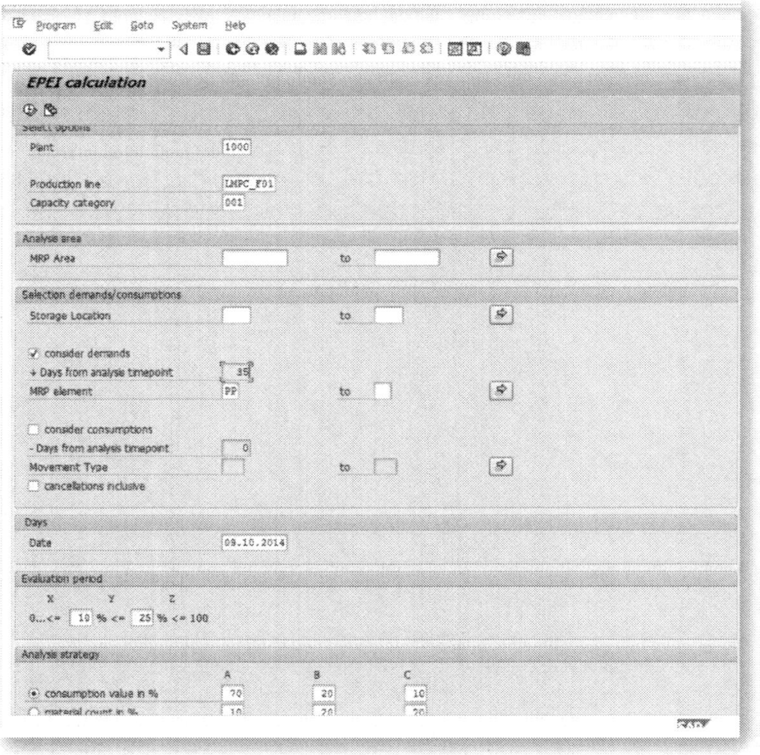

Figure 3.31: Initial selection screen for the EPEI calculation

Once the scope of the portfolio and the boundaries have been maintained, the result of the calculation is displayed, as in Figure 3.32.

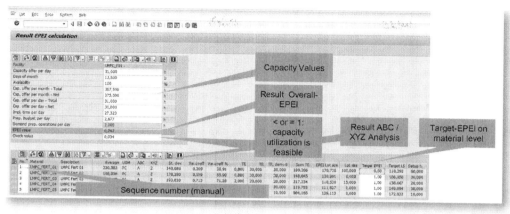

Figure 3.32: Result screen for the EPEI calculation

The upper section of Figure 3.32 shows summarized data of the entire portfolio, while the lower section shows the details. You can obtain valuable information from this, such as the ABC classification, EPEI numbers, capacity values and sequencing numbers.

From here we can use the EPEI result to branch off to the production schedule or rhythm wheel (product wheel). The LMPC offers a graphical display of the schedule in Figure 3.33.

You can see that groups of materials are assigned, with their production quantities, to weekdays in the frozen zone. This schedule provides you with detailed start and end dates for each material according to an equal distribution of production with small lot sizes throughout the week (in this case, the frozen zone).

The schedule can be further evaluated and maintained in a graphical planning board. Figure 3.34 shows the enhanced graphical planning board of the LMPC. The standard planning board (CM25) has been enhanced in the LMPC by the addition of a table (ALV grid) that enables the detailed evaluation of each order.

141

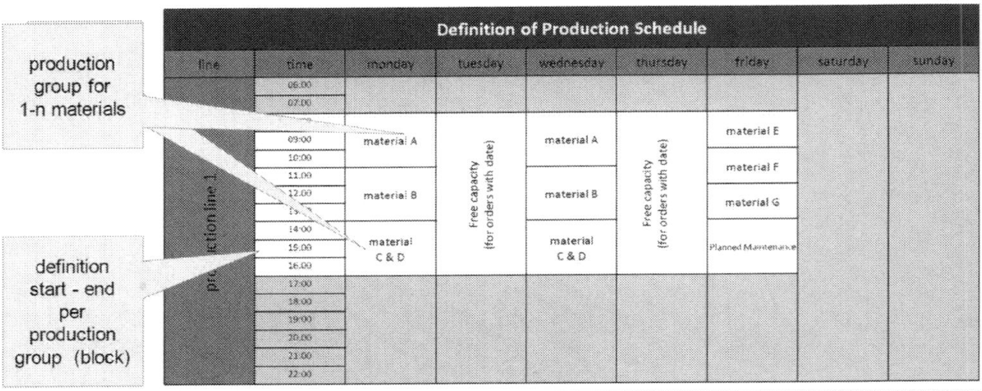

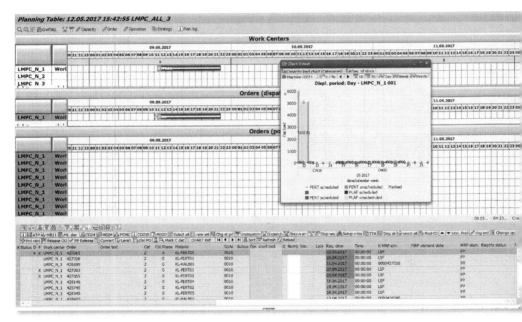

Figure 3.33: Rhythm wheel—production schedule

Figure 3.34: LMPC graphical planning board with ALV grid

Rhythm wheel (product wheel) scheduling offers an important alternative for generating a smooth production program that adheres to both lean (avoiding the waste from overproduction) as well as agile (flexible, demand-driven schedules) principles. The SAP Add-On Tool LMPC is an efficient tool for managing and setting up rhythm wheels in SAP without the need to resort to 3rd party work-arounds.

3.7 Kanban

'Kanban' is one of those buzzwords that have become synonymous with 'pull' production. Moreover, when people talk about lean they often refer to Kanban as the solution. In fact, Kanban is a consumption-based replenishment method—meaning that you need to hold inventory without demand and that the quantity you hold can be based on your past consumption pattern. However, unlike a reorder level procedure (another consumption-based replenishment method), the replenishment signal isn't triggered by inventory management in SAP, but rather by a visually-controlled inventory void in a pre-defined container.

In SAP, Kanban can immediately generate a replenishment order without the need to run MRP (as is the case in a reorder point procedure).

SAP offers the ability to create a Kanban control cycle for a material which has a demand side and a supply side for the inventory necessary to fulfill the Kanban method. There are two graphical screens that illustrate the demand side (see Figure 3.35) and the supply side (see Figure 3.36).

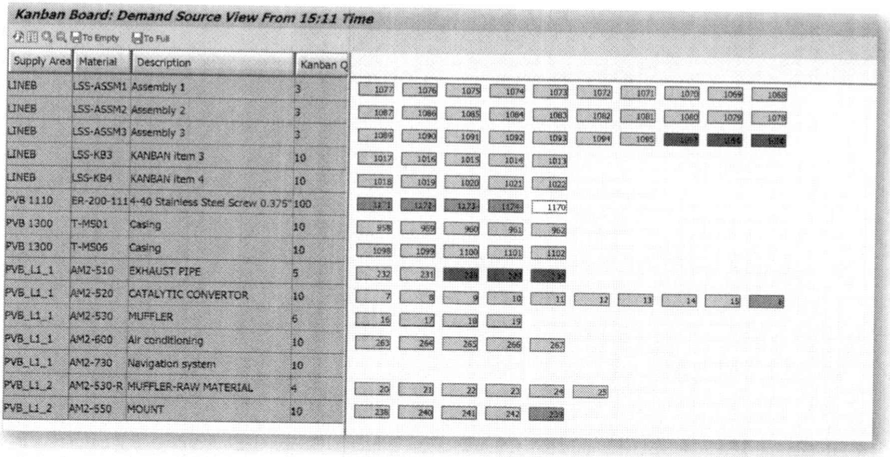

Figure 3.35: Kanban demand board view

143

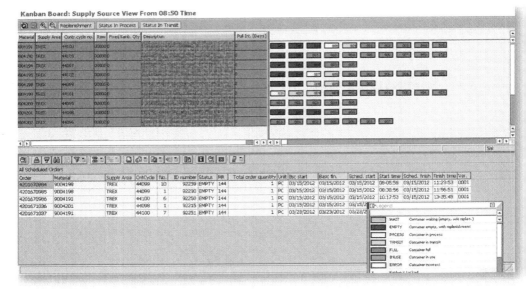

Figure 3.36: Kanban supply source view

You can use these screens to set containers to 'empty' or 'full', communicate what's being worked on or just get an overview of the situation.

Kanban is not really a scheduling method. In fact, it is just a method to generate replenishment orders without putting them in sequence or leveling them within available capacity. Therefore, if you want to use Kanban, you must provide a capacity buffer at the supply source that can take the orders coming from a Kanban void.

3.8 conWIP

In their groundbreaking book 'Factory Physics', Spearman and Hopp conceptualized the conWIP system (constant work in process) as an alternative to Kanban. They describe a push system as one where output is controlled (scheduled) and WIP is observed. Conversely, a pull system is defined by its control of the WIP level and the observation of the output rate. We can say that a pull system limits the amount of WIP that is in the system at any given point in time. In other words, a WIP cap is forced upon the system.

Using that definition, Kanban is a pull system because it allows only a certain number of cards to be in the system and therefore does not allow a WIP buildup. Depending on the amount of stations and operations on a production line, a possible disadvantage of a Kanban system is that there might be many Kanban control cycles and each control cycle is managed by cards; the resulting amount of WIP might be rather large.

A conWIP system provides a solution to that very problem. A conWIP system could also be called a one-card Kanban system because what comes out of the line at the end sends signals to the beginning of the line, avoiding all the cycles in the middle. What's important to note is that if nothing comes out at the end, nothing is released into the line at the beginning. This ensures WIP control. If WIP builds up on the line, nothing comes out at the end and, therefore, nothing goes onto the line. WIP can only build up so much.

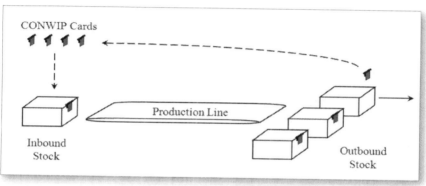

Figure 3.37: A conWIP system

In Figure 3.37, we can see a conWIP where, unlike Kanban which re-quires inventory at every reporting point, conWIP spans multiple levels along the production line and sends signals from the demand source across multiple stations to a point where orders are being 'pushed' through the system. The signal 'pulls' from the source, but the pull doesn't go from source to source looking for inventory at every point. Instead, it goes to the first (of many) sources and releases a set of or-ders, which it pushes into the line in a sequence to fulfill the demand and fill the container to 'full' again.

One way to configure this into SAP is by way of the special 'direct pro-duction' procurement type (type 52 in the MRP2 screen), which creates and schedules a collective order. Make sure your lot sizes are set to EX with no minimum or maximum so that the conWIP cycle has a consistent batch quantity.

Another way could be to create of a routing that spans the entire produc-tion line without the need to put goods issues and goods receipts be-tween orders. In this case, you would run the signals through a Kanban control cycle from the end of the line (demand source) to the beginning of the line (supply source).

Unlike Kanban, conWIP deals well with a wide variety of products found, for example, in a make-to-order environment. Since conWIP has no part number assigned, any part can be assigned temporarily when the de-mand occurs.

Another advantage of conWIP over Kanban is that there is less WIP required in a conWIP system. Spearman claims that because there are less cards in one conWIP system than there are in multiple Kanban con-trol cycles, WIP only collects at the bottleneck and not, as in Kanban, throughout the entire production line.

In any case, consider conWIP as another option in your toolbox for opti-mizing your production scheduling. It's well worth exploring further.

3.9   Rate-based scheduling of a flow line

Rate-based scheduling is a greatly underutilized feature in companies using SAP software to do capacity planning. In fact, for many of the schedules where rate-based planning would be a great feature, the planners and schedulers resort to Excel spreadsheets. Often this is due to misunderstanding how to set up and use rate-based planning in SAP and also because a spreadsheet naturally supports rate planning and its inherent structure.

Rate-based planning means planning quantities within periods. Rate-based planning does **not** mean using start and end dates of orders, but rather summing up the supply (given by planned orders) that is neces-sary to meet a given demand in a certain period, and planning by moving around the quantities from period to period until the schedule is leveled to stay within available capacity.

In SAP, transaction MF50 is a planning table within which you can perform rate-based planning (Transaction CM25 is not). As you can see in Figure 3.38, you can select the scheduling level and capacity planning in the initial screen.

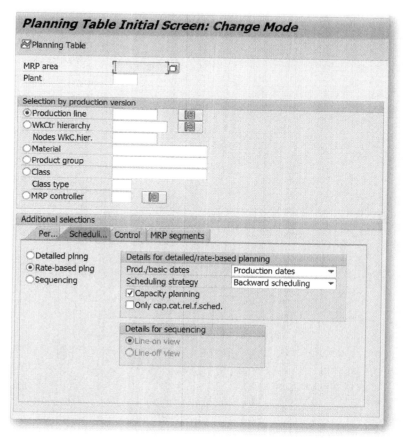

Figure 3.38: MF50—select rate-based planning and capacity planning

In the PERIOD tab we can also select whether we want to plan in daily, weekly or monthly buckets. However, this can be changed once you plan within MF50.

After you select the plant, production line and period you want to schedule, the rate-based planning grid will be displayed and is ready for scheduling, as shown in Figure 3.39.

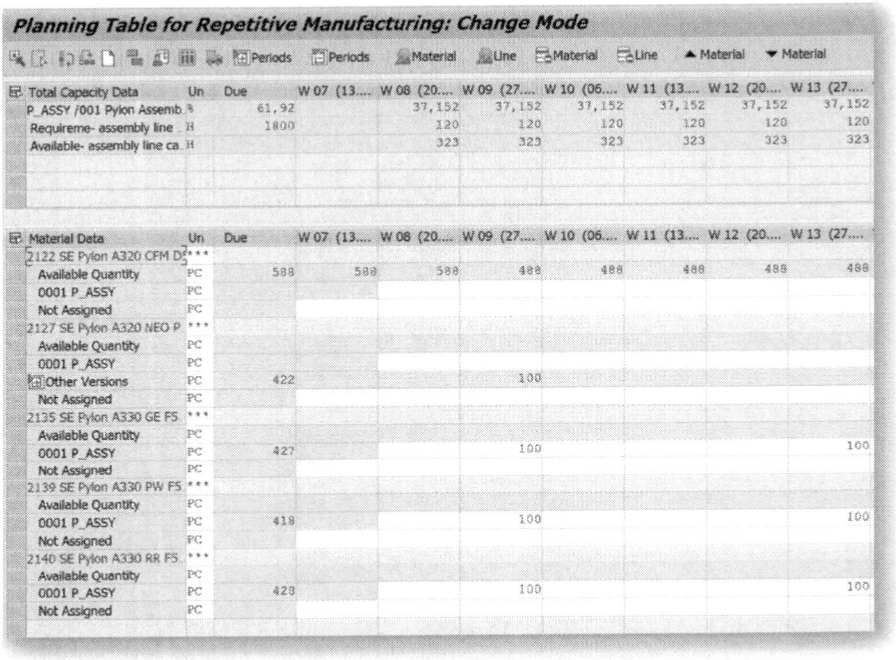

Figure 3.39: Rate-based planning with MF50

This looks like an Excel spreadsheet, doesn't it?

MF50 accumulates the quantities from planned orders in the same period (days, months or weeks) and displays the total in their respective cells. The cumulative capacity load for all orders and the available capacity hours from the production line are then displayed in the top row (required capacity hours). Therefore, the system is able to calculate the capacity utilization for various periods (daily, weekly, monthly—whichever you prefer).

As you type a quantity into an empty cell for a specific product, the system automatically generates a planned order and the capacity load created by the order, and displays the new situation on top.

There are many distribution and leveling functions available in MF50 (see the various menus) that you can play around with. These make it possible to automatically level to 80% utilization or distribute quantities evenly over periods and shifts.

Rate-based **scheduling** is far more suitable for packaging lines, filling lines and general flow lines than detailed scheduling will ever be. But be aware that rate-based **planning** is useful for discrete manufacturers too. For example, consider the production of sub-assemblies for aircraft where the elementary parts that go into the sub-assembly are discretely scheduled. You can check and plan the load on your machining shop by rate-based planning the sub-assembly for the medium term—e.g. 8 weeks to 6 months out.

This will help you to decide how much work you can do on your own shop floor and how much work you have to outsource to external manufacturers.

To use this feature, you must set up production versions for the products you want to plan in this way. The scheduling levels can be set within the production version; the scheduling levels for medium-term planning can be different to those for short-term planning.

The setup in the production version looks like the example shown in Figure 3.40.

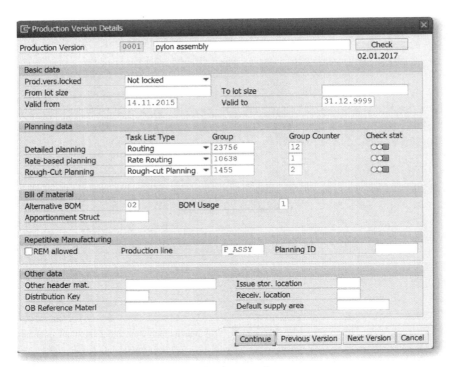

Figure 3.40: Detail screen of a production version

Note that in the production version you have the ability to use three different task lists on three different scheduling levels. This means complete flexibility in long-term, medium-term and short-term planning. In this example, we've used a standard routing at the detailed planning level, a rate routing at the rate-based planning level and a rough-cut planning profile at the rough-cut planning level.

You can translate this into long, medium and short-term planning levels if you set customizing in customizing transaction OPU5 (for planned orders) accordingly. This is detailed in Figure 3.41.

Plant	1007	bigbyte
Order type	LA	Stock order
Prodn Superv.	150	3 scheduling levels

☐ Long-term planning

Detailed Scheduling

| Sched. hor.det. | 40 | | ☑ Scheduling |
| SelID: Detailed | 01 | | ☑ Generate Capacity Reqs. |

Rate-Based Scheduling

| Rate.plng horzn | 120 | | ☑ Scheduling |
| SelID:rate plng | 02 | | ☑ Generate Capacity Reqs. |

Rough-Cut Scheduling

| RCutPlg horizon | 480 | | ☑ Scheduling |
| SelID:roughPlng | 02 | | ☑ Generate Capacity Reqs. |

Sequencing

☑ Takt Time/Rate-Based Sched.

Adjust Scheduling

Scheduling Level	Via rate-based scheduling	▼
Adjust Dates	Adjust basic dates, adjust dep. reqmts to operation date	▼
In Capacity Scheduling	Always basic dates, dep.reqmts to operation dates	▼

Scheduling Control for Detailed Scheduling

Scheduling Type	Backwards ▼	☐ Automatic Log
Start in the Past		☐ Latest Staging Date
		☐ Scheduling with Breaks

Reduction

Reduction Type	All operations in the order will be reduced	▼
Maximum Reduction Level	Do not reduce	▼
	L1 L2 L3 L4 L5 L6	
% Reduction in Floats		

Figure 3.41: Customizing planning levels for short, medium and long-term planning

This type of customization allows you to decide what type of task list (standard routing, rate routing, recipe, etc.) to use for the various levels (through the selection ID), how far in advance planned orders are to be generated by the MRP Run using this task list type (scheduling horizon in working days), and whether scheduling should be carried out and capacity requirements generated.

In Figure 3.41, the general scheduling level has been set to rate-based which allows you to call up transaction MF50 (the planning table) with rate-based planning. If you start the MRP Run with lead time scheduling, it also means that the planned orders that were generated by the MRP Run will include rate records (beside the detailed scheduling records).

This provides a very flexible basis for scheduling your product spectrum through the various planning horizons. My general recommendation is to perform rate-based scheduling in the long-term and medium-term horizons but detailed, time-based scheduling in the short term. This ensures that you effectively level capacities throughout all periods.

3.10 Drum-Buffer-Rope

Drum-Buffer-Rope (DBR) is a scheduling solution stemming from the Theory of Constraints, which evolved from Eliyahu Goldratt's philosophies. The fundamental assumption of DBR is that in any plant there is only one or maybe a limited number of bottleneck resources which control the overall output of that plant.

This is the 'drum' which dictates the pace for all other resources. Scheduling and execution behaviors are focused on exploiting the drum in order to maximize the output of the system and protect it against variability through the use of 'buffers'; thereby synchronizing all other resources to the activity of the drum through a mechanism that is like a 'rope'.

In order to set up a Drum-Buffer-Rope scheduling system in SAP, you must combine standard components to act like it. There are many ways to do this. The one I implemented at a customer in the process industry is detailed below.

As the name implies, a Drum-Buffer-Rope system has a drum from which the pace is signaled, a buffer that serves as protection and a rope that 'pulls' in the previous operations. This concept is illustrated in Figure 3.42.

Figure 3.42: A Drum-Buffer-Rope system

My customer is runs a manufacturing line where raw materials are pre-processed in an oven and then processed in bulk before the bulk is mixed into finished and packaged products. The bottleneck turned out to be the last processing step. Figure 3.43 shows a LEGO® model of the production line—the bottleneck is indicated by an arrow.

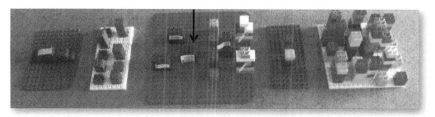

Figure 3.43: LEGO® model of the production line with indication of the bottleneck

It was extremely important not to overload the machine but to keep it running constantly. Therefore, we decided to schedule the line with a Drum-Buffer-Rope system that kept the bottleneck busy because it was scheduled as the pacesetter. At the same time, the bottleneck was pro-tected with a buffer of inventory right before the bottleneck. The packag-ing operation then pulled the buffer inventory into the bottleneck.

This setup is shown in Figure 3.44.

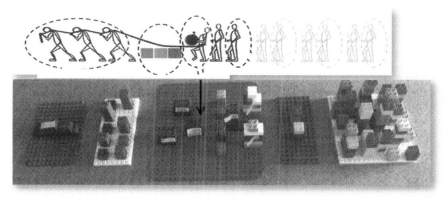

Figure 3.44: Assigning the drum to the bottleneck and pulling through the protective inventory buffer

The whole system was then configured into SAP. First, raw materials replenishment policies were developed and assigned after segmentation of the portfolio. The buffer inventory before the bottleneck was driven by a component forecast (requirements type VSFB), and the buffer inventory after the bottleneck was set up using Kanban control cycles. The bottleneck itself was scheduled using the product wheel method which we configured as a profile into transaction CM25. Finally, the packaging lines pulled with a takt-based schedule that was triggered with customer Kanbans that attached themselves to the planned orders in the schedule.

The entire system is depicted in Figure 3.45.

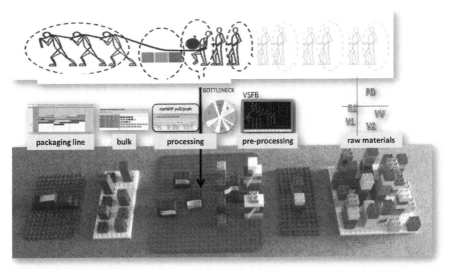

Figure 3.45: The Drum-Buffer-Rope system configured into standard SAP

As you can see, the entire system was configured using only standard SAP functionality. No work-arounds, additional development or third-party tools were required.

Using SAP software this way is not limited to just Drum-Buffer-Rope. The software offers a wide variety of functions that let you schedule in almost every way possible when combined and used properly.

As we all know, production scheduling and capacity planning falls short during implementation of SAP software because it is considered difficult to properly design and there is often a lack of knowledge about its features. However, it's well worth the effort to take a second look once things have calmed down.

4 Outlook 2020 and beyond

At the time of writing this book, there are numerous SAP products under various licensing agreements on the market. There is capacity management functionality in the SAP ERP offering, namely within the PP module, and there is PP/DS (Production Planning and Detailed Scheduling) in SAP's APO. As of now, it is not really clear—at least not to the public—what will be coming with S/4 HANA and/or IBP (Integrated Business Planning). The information is vague at best and only leaves room for speculation.

In this book, I have specifically focused on SAP ERP because this is the only 'sure shot' towards what the future will bring and is therefore currently the only sensible and effective recommendation I can give. There are rumors that PP/DS will be rolled into IBP, but there are also rumors that PP/DS, and all of APO, will disappear and IBP will be a brand new offering. But then again, we don't exactly know what is coming with IBP either.

So much for an outlook, right?

Well, all this confusion is the major reason I wrote this book about SAP ERP and its capabilities—to help you manage your resources. And to be honest, when only a fraction of companies using SAP truly utilize SAP ERP to do capacity planning, why would organizations jump into something new they don't really know anything about?

In the end, to perform effective, efficient, integrated and automated capacity management you need a tool that can host master data for capacity availability; generate capacity requirements; and sequence, level and schedule orders in a system that is connected to costing, sales forecasting and materials management.

SAP ERP has all that and more. What are you waiting for?

Uwe Goehring, New York, NY, January 24, 2017

ESPRESSO TUTORIALS

You have finished the book.

A   About the Author

Uwe Goehring is an SAP Mentor and has worked in supply chain optimization for more than 20 years. He is the founder and president of bigbyte software systems corporation, which optimizes SAP supply chains around the world by coaching planners, buyers, and schedulers in policy setting and strategic and tactical planning.

B   Index

C Disclaimer

This publication contains references to the products of SAP SE.

SAP, R/3, SAP NetWeaver, Duet, PartnerEdge, ByDesign, SAP Busi-nessObjects Explorer, StreamWork, and other SAP products and ser-vices mentioned herein as well as their respective logos are trademarks or registered trademarks of SAP SE in Germany and other countries.

Business Objects and the Business Objects logo, BusinessObjects, Crystal Reports, Crystal Decisions, Web Intelligence, Xcelsius, and other Business Objects products and services mentioned herein as well as their respective logos are trademarks or registered trademarks of Busi-ness Objects Software Ltd. Business Objects is an SAP company.

Sybase and Adaptive Server, iAnywhere, Sybase 365, SQL Anywhere, and other Sybase products and services mentioned herein as well as their respective logos are trademarks or registered trademarks of Sybase, Inc. Sybase is an SAP company.

SAP SE is neither the author nor the publisher of this publication and is not responsible for its content. SAP Group shall not be liable for errors or omissions with respect to the materials. The only warranties for SAP Group products and services are those that are set forth in the express warranty statements accompanying such products and services, if any. Nothing herein should be construed as constituting an additional warranty.

More Espresso Tutorials Books

Claudia Jost:

First Steps in the SAP® Purchasing Processes (MM)

► Compact manual for the SAP procurement processes

► Comprehensive example with numerous illustrations

► Master data, purchase requirements and goods receipt in context

http://5016.espresso-tutorials.com

Björn Weber:

First Steps in the SAP® Production Processes (PP)

► Compact manual for discrete production in SAP

► Comprehensive example with numerous illustrations

► Master data, resource planning and production orders in context

http://5027.espresso-tutorials.com

Stephen Birchall:

Invoice Verification for SAP®

▶ Learn everything you need for invoice verification and its role in FI and MM

▶ Keep user input to a minimum and automate the process

▶ Discover best practices to configure and maximize the use of this function

http://5073.espresso-tutorials.com

Kevin Riddell, Rajen Iyver:

Practical Guide to SAP® GTS, Part 1: SPL Screening and Compliance Management

▶ Tips and tricks for leveraging SAP GTS to automate trade compliance

▶ Walk step by step through business processes

▶ Overview of regulatory requirements and compliance suggestions

▶ Review of Version 11.0 with screenshots

http://5100.espresso-tutorials.com

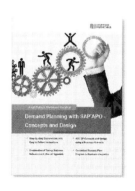

Avijt Dutta & Shreekant Shiralkar:

Demand Planning with SAP® APO—Concepts and Design

▶ Step-by-Step Explanations and Easy to Follow Instructions

▶ Combination of Theory, Business Relevance and 'How to' Approach

▶ APO DP Concepts and Design Explained using a Business Scenario

▶ Centralized Process Flow Diagram to Illustrate Integration

http://5105.espresso-tutorials.com

Avijt Dutta & Shreekant Shiralkar:

Demand Planning with SAP® APO—Execution

► Step-by-Step Explanations and Easy to Follow Instructions

► Combination of Theory, Business Relevance and 'How to' Approach

► APO DP Execution Explained using a Business Scenario

► Centralized Process Flow Diagram to Illustrate Integration

http://5106.espresso-tutorials.com

Tobias Götz, Anette Götz:

Practical Guide to SAP® Transportation Management (2nd edition)

► Supported business processes

► Best practices

► Integration aspects and architecture

► Comparison and differentiation to similar SAP components

http://5082.espresso-tutorials.com

Matthew Johnson:

SAP® Material Master—A Practical Guide

► Understand SAP Master concepts

► Maximize your value stream through SAP Materials Management (MM)

► Walk through practical implementation examples

http://5028.espresso-tutorials.com

Made in the USA
Lexington, KY
28 June 2018